My Vanishing
African Dreams

By Susan M. Hall

Strategic Book Publishing and Rights Co.

Strategic Book Publishing and Rights Co., LLC
USA I Singapore

For information about special discounts for bulk purchases, please contact Strategic Book Publishing and Rights Co. Special Sales, at bookorder@sbpra.net.

ISBN: 978-1-68181-850-4

Book Design: Suzanne Kelly

DEDICATION

For my parents, Thelma and John,
to whom I owe so much.

Acknowledgements

My sincere thanks go to the following people:
My parents, Thelma and John, for reading through my manuscript as I wrote each chapter; Thurl Jackson, for typing my handwritten work; Mohamed Ismail, for helping me find a publisher and reading through my manuscript, and giving me moral support and advice; Vincent Ford, for formatting the text into Word, ready to send to the publisher; and Vicki and Allen Stanton, for moral support and advice. I would also like to thank Stefanie Powers, for her kindness in forwarding my book.

Without the help from family and friends, this book would never have been completed.

FOREWORD

I recall meeting Susan Hall and her parents in the mid-1970s at the Settlers Store, a market/dry-goods shop in Nanyuki. Settlers was a local watering hole for people from all over the district who would come in to town to buy supplies, collect mail, and hear the latest gossip.

Susan's family was known as The Halls: "Have you met The Halls?" said the person who introduced us. Clearly, as with so many eccentric individualists who choose to live in isolated parts of Kenya, The Halls had a certain character that set them apart. In so many ways Kenya is a place where the unconventional is, in fact, conventional.

The unusual nature of Susan's life fits well with the means of expression in her writing. Her enthusiastic recounting of her adventures leaps off the page as it jumps from one exciting escapade to another. Her book is an entertaining read for an agile mind, and I hope others will relate to the joys of living in Kenya over those years as much as I did.

—Stefanie Powers

TABLE OF CONTENTS

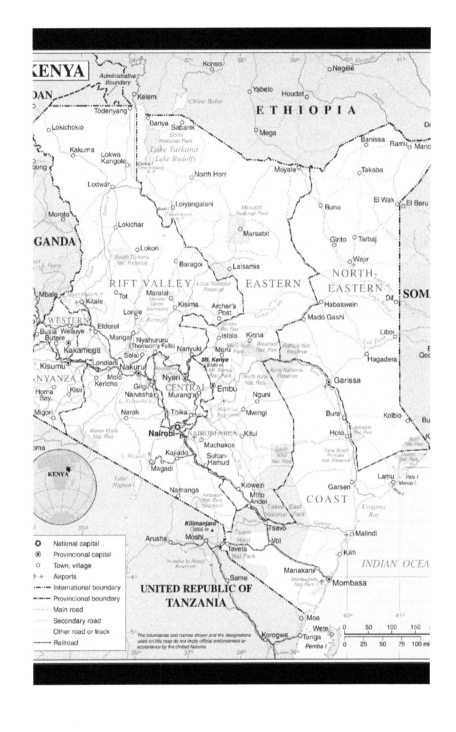

KENYA

Administrative Boundary

National capital
Provincial capital
Town, village
Airports
International boundary
Provincial boundary
Main road
Secondary road
Other road or track
Railroad

The boundaries and names shown and the designations
used on this map do not imply official endorsement or
acceptance by the United Nations.

PROLOGUE:
OUR ARRIVAL IN KENYA

Where my life and I were born
How soothing were the songs of dawn,
Is it a dream ... or do I hear ...
Africa ... Africa ... Africa calls ...
The throbbing of a heart so near?

—Susan M. Hall

The three-hundred-year-old farmhouse still stands alone, near Oxton Village, Nottinghamshire. I was born on the top floor of its three storeys on the 13th of July 1948. The first four and a half years of my life were spent on the farms my parents leased. Things were extremely difficult after the war, and my young parents decided to leave England for good.

My father's dream has always been of Africa, and so it was that in January 1953, we took off from Blackbush Airfield, in Southern England, in a thirty-seater, twin-engine Viking owned by Airwork and Hunting Clan, bound for Kenya, and piloted by Captain Philips, who we later learned was trained to fly by my grandfather, Captain Lewis Wigham Hall. My first recollection of this flight was looking out of the starboard windows and seeing sparks and flames shooting along the aircraft. It was dark, and the flames reflected glowing light into the cabin. We had taken off from Malta and were over the Mediterranean when the starboard engine erupted in flames. The crew managed, with difficulty, to extinguish the fire, but we were now flying on one engine, and the Viking could not fly very far with only one engine operating. We turned and headed back towards Malta, losing height rapidly, until the Viking was just skimming along the surface of the water. A fearful experience for my parents and all the other passengers and crew, as it looked as if the Viking would sink into the ocean before reaching the island. I, of course, was totally unaware of the grave danger we were all in.

We finally limped sluggishly into Malta and landed safely. Due to technical difficulties, we spent five days in Malta waiting for another aircraft to come from England. Taking off in the second Viking, we flew to Benghazi, on the northern tip of Africa, to refuel, and then on to Wadi Halfa, when another technical problem occurred. So we spent a night or two in Wadi Halfa on the banks of the river Nile. I remember the hotel where we stayed was very spartan and bleak. I was terrified of the tall, black Sudanese waiters, dressed in white kanzus and red fezzes. They didn't smile and had sullen looks on their dark faces as they all but threw the stone-hard bread rolls on to our side plates.

In a day or two we were airborne once more and headed for Khartoum, and then on to Juba, where we were to drop off a missionary family. When the cabin crew opened the aircraft door, waves of unbearable heat floated in. It was very hot, and the flight had been bumpy. Flying at only nine thousand feet, most passengers were sick, including me. Finally, we arrived at Embakasi Airfield in Nairobi. My parents had the sum of five pounds to their name, which was spent on a dress for my mother and a pair of trousers for my father, and so it was that we began a new and very exciting life.

For the next five years, my father was to manage a mixed farm in the Wanjohi Valley known as "Happy Valley." The farm belonged to Alistair Gibb and Partners. Soon after we arrived my brother, Andrew, was born. In 1958 we moved to Nderit Estate, a thirty-thousand-acre cattle ranch, situated on the shore of Lake Nakuru, a lake world famous for its millions of flamingos in the Great Rift Valley. The four of us lived on the beautiful ranch, adorned with wildlife and birds, my father being the manager at that time.

I did a limited number of years' school education at Nakuru Boarding School, which I hated; being away from home and family life did not suit me at all, and my health deteriorated considerably. When Nakuru School was closed down in January 1963 due to lack of pupils, I was given two choices: going overseas to further my education, or staying in Kenya to help build up the new ranch that my parents were buying near Nanyuki. I would have to be prepared to work very hard, learn all about cattle trading, and, to a great extent, educate myself. I was thirteen years old at the time. I decided to stay.

PART ONE
ENASOIT, THE RANCH OF WONDER

THE LION ATTACK

In the early evening there comes a knock upon the door;
I hear excited voices calling
Simba! Simba! They cry.

—Thelma G. Hall

Golden shafts of light streamed through the billowing clouds of red dust as the African sun dipped towards the hazy horizon. A herd of just over two-hundred head of sleek Boran steers headed for the boma (livestock enclosure), their dewlaps swaying from side to side, their humps quivering with each step as they loped along. Wrinkles of soft skin surrounded their eyes. One or two of them turned to look at me as they passed, their bellies full after another day of grazing in the scrub bush country.

The herdsman of the Boran tribe, Kini Ebrahim Osman, flashed a wide, friendly smile at me, his white teeth evenly shaped and shining. His eyes, bloodshot from the day's dust, were set in an ebony face of high cheekbones, and a turban of faded red check was perched askew on his head. "Jambo Susanna," he called. He wore a tattered, khaki bush-shirt and a pair of trousers made into long shorts frayed at the edges. A pair of worn sandals made from old car tyre remains covered his dusty, gnarled feet, with toenails broken from a life in rough semi-desert country. A shotgun slung casually over one shoulder. This was just one of the herds of cattle coming into the night enclosure on Enasoit Ranch, and this group was mine. I felt very proud, watching my own stock and the herder who worked for me, disappear over the brow of the hill in the fading light of another African dusk.

***

It was two in the morning and the night was warm and still. I heard a gunshot, and then another. It could only be our cattle night guard, and the sound came in through my open bedroom window from the direction of the night bomas. I called through to my father, who was breathing rhythmically next to my mother in their nearby bedroom. In no time he was up and out, with his Winchester 30-30 Saddle Carbine, into the Land Rover and away down to the bomas. The cattle had burst through the thorn bush-made enclosure where they slept and were scattered all over the countryside. Then pug prints in the dust were seen around the boma, from a number of young lions by the size of the spoor.

Suddenly, there was a blood-curdling growl, and then a roar, as three young lions leaped out from behind a nearby bush and bounded into the darkness of a star-studded night. All the stock-men came out of their adobe huts at the sound of the growls, shots and bellowing, stampeding cattle. The shots were fired in the air to frighten off the beautiful, golden-coloured cats, and everyone rushed around trying to gather stock and return them to the boma, but it was totally impossible in the dark. The poor beasts were terrified by the scent of the lions—their eyes wide with fear, they dashed past everybody in total confusion, breathing heavily, and froth spewing from their nostrils. Any thought of trying to recover or count the cattle was abandoned and everyone returned to their houses, overpowered by excitement and too wide awake for sleep, hearts beating faster with no will to slow down.

The first glow in the eastern sky of dawn approached, and we were up and off to look for our scattered stock. Having counted them three or four times, we discovered fifteen head were missing. Then the search began.

Following the lions' spoor, we came upon the first of five dead steers. The three half-grown cubs were traumatised; their mother had been shot by a neighbouring rancher a few nights before. We were to learn this later, and the cubs killed the cattle because of it—they had only eaten the hindquarters of one steer. Being so upset by the loss of their mother provoked them into killing indiscriminately. Two of the five steers had an "SH" brand on them; they were mine. A financial loss perhaps, but I felt so dispirited, and my heart went out to those unfortunate cubs for their suffering.

Ten cattle were still missing but, after two days searching, we eventually found them bunched up together way up on the Lolldaiga Hills. One unfortunate animal had slipped, rolled part way down a rocky slope, and broken a hind leg. The poor beast could not walk and sat there looking totally despondent, knowing death was imminent. The men slaughtered it on the spot. The meat was carried down by the herdsmen, who slipped and slid their way down the steep hillside, the fresh, dripping red meat slung over their shoulders. They later shared it amongst themselves and ate with great relish that evening.

ENASOIT

This Africa so fierce and strong
Is like the beating of a gong.
It has always nurtured me;
There—Forever, I will be.

—Thelma G. Hall

Enasoit ("the place of many rocks," in the Massai language) was ten thousand acres of beautiful country suitable for ranching, with an abundance of wildlife, a piece of the most fabulous looking country in Africa. We needed our own land to run stock, to make a living, to make a life. The temptation to own this scenic wonder, a treasure and most desirable composition of God's own country, was too great to lose.

Tall, red oat grass waved gently in the north-eastern breeze, rich brown in colour. The attractively outlined shape of the Lolldaiga Hills was a backdrop standing majestically against the cobalt sky. Outcrops of granite rocks formed appealing little kopjes with fig trees growing between the boulders, their roots stretching down to eventually reach the ground. Flocks of African brown parrots feeding on the tiny half-ripe figs flew out screeching their metallic calls to one another. Plains with acacia trees grew along the winding gullies, and beneath their canopies of shade stood little groups of Burchell's zebra, resting in the midday heat, their tails swishing to and fro, keeping the flies off their shapely flanks; they lifted their heads with an almost arrogant air. Tall, slender, reticulated giraffe nibbled the last of the tiny green leaves from the tops of the acacia trees before the greenery finally dried and dropped to the ground unable to survive in the scorching sun any longer. A number of giraffe

6

cantered off and stopped fifty yards away to turn and look, their enormous eyes fringed by long lashes, and they proudly turned away to continue feeding gracefully.

Small herds of impala stood lazily around a little water hole close by. Dust spiralled up in funnels and was whirled along by the hot wind. Some of the water holes were beginning to dry out leaving muddy wallows in which the warthogs enjoyed rolling their hot plump bodies.

This was our first viewing of the land we would buy in 1962. During the 1960s, Columbia Pictures arrived on the property. They spent seven months and made part of the film *Born Free* on our land, so Enasoit was seen on screen by millions of people around the globe. Forty-three years later, I never ceased to be enthralled by this gem of wonder, which has been our home during many difficult, and sometimes sad, but also brilliantly happy and enchanting times.

THE MOVE

Moving from the lakeside
To the hills at Enasoit
Do our hearts pine for the shores …
Or … Rejoice with what we've sought?
                                        —Susan M. Hall.

W̶e moved to Enasoit in March 1963. The land, its plains
dotted with "whistling" thorn trees, is twenty-two miles
north of the little town of Nanyuki, our closest shopping centre.
Nanyuki sits almost on the equator just below the immensity
of Mount Kenya, its craggy, snow-covered peaks rising to over
seventeen thousand feet above sea level.

The second-hand Land Rover was bought to move to the
new ranch. Heavily loaded with household effects—books,
shelves, a small chest of drawers, bedding and cushions, boxes
filled with various goods—it was sent off with our driver,
Lakaken, bound for Enasoit, a 145-mile drive from Nderit.

Later the same evening we received an urgent message
from the Thomson's Falls (as it was called then) Police Station.
Lakaken was on the phone. This was very ominous, as he should
have arrived at Enasoit by this time. "*Gari na kwisha, na kwisha
kabisa,*" he said: the vehicle is finished, completely and utterly.
He sounded unusually cheerful in his excitement, considering
what we were about to learn.

Five miles out of Thomson's Falls, driving far too fast,
Lakaken had skidded in thick, gluey mud, hit a ditch, then a
bank, and rolled the Land Rover five times. It was a total write
off, hence "*Gari na kwisha kabisa.*" Miraculously, no one was
hurt.

Our belongings were strewn far and wide, all in the pouring rain. Books were damaged, as some of the boxes had burst open. One of the drawers was missing from the chest, never to be found. Everything was collected up and dumped at the police station in a jumbled heap.

A small, privately owned garage in Ol Joro Orok offered to buy the wreck for a pittance, but we decided to get it back to Enasoit. The following year, Father and I began to slowly rebuild it, buying second-hand parts from Grogan Road in Nairobi. Grogan Road, named after the explorer Ewart Scott Grogan, is a back street of Nairobi, with shops selling all kinds of spare parts, some second-hand, some possibly even stolen. If there was something in the way of vehicle spares you weren't able to get anywhere else, you would always find them down Grogan Road. I remember a man once telling us that he went down there one day to buy two new headlamps for his old Land Rover. The shopkeeper asked him to sit down and relax with a cup of coffee while he organised everything. After what seemed rather a long time, the headlamps arrived and were duly packed in a box. The man was delighted to get what he had set out to find, gave his thanks to the shopkeeper and, with a broad smile on his face, marched off back down the street to his Land Rover, only to find both headlamps on his car missing!

Two weeks after the Land Rover misfortune, we were bringing the last load of our possessions to Enasoit in the Wolseley 6/99. Cream with a maroon roof, it looked very fashionable and was one of the few two-tone cars around at the time, an upmarket family saloon with gorgeous maroon leather seats and walnut dashboard.

One day, out of a rolling cloud of white dust came a bright-red station wagon, like a monster, its chrome bumper bar glinting in the intense sunlight. It was overtaking an army lorry and descending upon us at high speed along the Naibor Road. Unable to move out of the way in time, it swerved violently, hit us with crushing force, and smashed the right wing of our car, which propelled us sideways across the road, where we came to a halt. It was an immense shock, a very undermining experience for the beginning of a new life, but this was not to be the end of our misfortune.

***

She started losing height about sixty-five feet above the end of the airstrip just after take-off. Her engine changed tune. Mother and I looked at one another in total horror. "We're not going to make it," she whispered, as I clung to my seat with both hands in sickening fear, perspiration breaking out on my forehead.

A princess amongst them all, there was no aircraft more graceful than the Beechcraft Bonanza, a sleek beauty with V-shaped tail. Her stylish body painted red and white and trimmed with black, in the utmost of streamlined designs, sat atop her elegant but strong wings. Her retractable undercarriage was electrically operated as were her flaps. She was most certainly a picture of complete perfection, and a great joy of my father's life.

The searing and screeching sound of tearing metal created a deafening crescendo as we hurtled through the whistling thorn trees at sixty miles per hour and crashed to the ground, the propeller ripping its way through the undergrowth and tree trunks, the blades twisting into an ugly misshapen bow. VP-KHU was her registration, and she was being propelled along on her belly by what was left of her engine power. We were flung from side to side in our seats, the belts cutting into our thighs, our heads bumping against the side windows. Her airframe roared over stumps and bush, lunging from tree to tree, as her wings slammed trunks and twisted into a gnarled, screwed-up mass of unrecognisable metal. One hundred and fifty yards further on, she finally jerked to an abrupt halt. Switching off the ignition, my father, who was the pilot, opened the door and asked us to get out as fast as we could and run from VP-KHU in case she burst into flames. Shocked and stunned, but strangely not seriously injured, we stumbled out and moved away. When we were sure that VP-KHU was not going to blow up in flames, we walked back to have a look at the mangled, twisted wreck. There she lay, like a wounded bird, shot from the blue African sky.

I wept hot tears of despair, my head whirling with confusion, numb with shock and mentally paralyzed. I exchanged glances with my father and mother, who were in the same state. Father put his arms around us. "Don't cry, Lovey. We will get her rebuilt," he said to me. Within a moment or two after scrutinising the shrunken wreck once again, we realised with shock and hopelessness that the idea was completely out of the question: one wing had been ripped off totally, right up to the fuel tank, leaving the rubber lining gaping, just the stump left, like a jagged tooth. The wing was forty yards away from the wreckage and entirely wrapped around a tree. The fuselage was almost in two. We were extremely fortunate that the cabin had been so strong. Had we flown in any other aircraft, we would not have lived to relate this story. VP-KHU was now dead, dead for all time, never to leave the ground again, and, in her dying, she had saved us. She was to remain within our hearts forever. She had been a friend and companion, and we would miss her most dreadfully. Then the sound of an engine approached, grinding its way along the track, the one and only vehicle that was left: the old Dodge lorry. Our headman and house staff heard the horrendous noise of the crash and were on their way to the rescue. I held my little Maltese terrier in my arms, while he looked about in wonder and confusion, probably thinking we had reached our destination much sooner than expected.

The crash occurred in June 1963, only three months after we moved to the ranch. We were heading to Nairobi to collect my brother, Andrew, from school. Many, many years later, we were to learn the cause of the accident when the owner of an aircraft business at Wilson Airport bought the engine of VP-KHU and overhauled it. He'd discovered that a piston arm had snapped. This must have happened just after take-off, even though VP-KHU recently had her check-three Certificate of Airworthiness.

THE HOMESTEADS

Old wooden house
You have been my home
Then I moved to a
"Fairy Castle" of stone

— Susan M. Hall

The old wooden, rambling farmhouse had been badly eaten by termites; the soft board walls, painted in a soft powder blue, were totally chewed away, and soil tunnels full of little white ant-type creatures wound their way up to the ceiling. The house had to be sprayed with a solution made up for destroying these destructive termites, otherwise they would eventually eat the entire house, and it would crumble into dust.

Within a few weeks of moving in, we stripped all the old soft board away and lined the walls with papyrus matting. The tall, thick, grassy reeds, with their big pom-pom heads, grow on the shores of the vast inland sea of Lake Victoria. The people who live close to the lake in Western Kenya, stitch together the long, thick stems to form a mat, having removed the big fluffy heads. When freshly made, the mats are a gentle green in colour, turning to yellowish brown as they dry out. They turn out to be about six feet in width and eight feet long. The mats make a very attractive lining for walls and ceilings.

We bought all second-hand furniture—dining table and chairs, cupboards and wardrobes, cushions, easy chairs—when we first came to Enasoit from farm sales; sometimes one would buy a whole lot of small items on sale as one lot just to get one particular thing. Almost everything would be sold for a few shillings. People who were selling up at the time were desperate to get rid of all their belongings because of disturbances within the country. Many Europeans were leaving Kenya to look for homes and properties in other parts of the world, being uncertain of their future, for the country was to become an independent state.

We and a number of others chose to stay in this spellbinding country—a magnet from which we could never be drawn away. Land was selling very cheaply, so we decided to buy. It would be the best decision for us as a family.

The house had a corrugated iron roof. It had once been an Army married quarters in Nanyuki during the Second World War; later it had been bought up and transported to its present position by the previous landowner. These people were amongst those who had left the country, so the house had been empty for a number of years. It had a long narrow veranda that we decorated with potted plants; palms with tall fronds gracefully waved in the breeze, while trailing creepers of "Golden Shower" and "Dutchman's Pipe" curled their long stems around wooden support posts, giving a cool and colourful appearance that was greatly inviting to all who visited. The lawns were extensive, green in the rainy season but very dry and brown in the hot and sunny times.

At one end of the garden we had built a wall out of small granite boulders, an area that surrounded an unusually shaped fish pond with a shallow waterfall cascading over the rocks down into the pool. There were reeds growing around the edges on tiny islands where weaver birds enjoyed plucking the stems and flying off to a selected nesting ground.

When we first moved in, the toilet was a hole in the ground known as a "long drop," about twelve feet deep with a wooden surround on the top. It was encased in a small wooden hut a short distance from the house. Its roof was overgrown with morning glory, a creeper covered with lilac-coloured flowers, where a snake was spending a considerable amount of its time— a spitting cobra! The underneath of the seat area had also been chewed away by termites during the absence of people; it didn't feel particularly safe, perched upon its rickety throne. This was soon changed to a more convenient flush toilet, installed inside the main house.

Our refrigerator was a fifty-year-old Electrolux, which we bought second-hand from one of the many farm sales. It operated on kerosene and worked very efficiently. There was a bore hole close by, around three hundred feet deep, which provided wonderfully crystal-clear water for the homestead, garden, stock, and all wildlife in our area. The cattle would come bounding up to the drinking trough to fill themselves with the mineralized water, which they loved, lifting their heads as the sparkling liquid dripped from their soft lips, a look of contentment on their faces.

Much of the equipment belonging to the land when we bought it had disappeared by the time we finally moved in—a toilet was found three miles away hidden deep in the bush, as was the bath. Milk churns and hundreds of readymade concrete building blocks were located in a neighbour's backyard! A number of beautiful wild horses and some cattle were also missing, never to be recovered.

Over the span of time, our settler-style residence became very comfortable, a pleasing and peaceful home for twenty-four years. After we had moved out of this charming old house, it was to play a small part in the film *Nowhere in Africa*.

In 1981, we started to build an enormous castle-style house, which took all of seven long years of extremely hard work to complete. Our family of four—my mother, father, brother Andrew, and I—were all involved with the designing of it.

Father taught a Kipsigis man how to do *fundi* (Swahili for mason) work and, under father's instructions, Kibor worked together with a couple of helpers, totally unskilled, and, together with our own input, the most unusual creation evolved.

The walls were built of granite boulders, roughly the size of a football, bound together with mud and mixed to a thick, gluey consistency with water. The red-clay type soil was dug out of the ground close by the building site. Later, as the building grew, it was pointed on the inside and outside with a cement mix, to hold the mud in place and a protection against the rain. It had a "crazy paving" effect and looked extremely attractive, as each boulder was a slightly different colour. The walls were two feet thick. Wide Moorish archways were created that led into the living and dining areas, giving a regal air and continuity to the spacious rooms.

This new home was nestled amongst huge granite boulders and outcrops of flattish rocks on an extensive kopje overlooking magnificent country with all the wildlife: graceful giraffe, rich rufous coloured eland, long-horned oryx, and many other varieties of plains game. Sometimes the dark shapes of buffalo and the huge phantoms of Africa (the elephants) could be seen drinking at a water hole below.

Mother, Father and I were heavily involved in a considerable amount of work being done on the building, a wonder rising out of the depths of the hillside of Enasoit. On the outside of the homestead, the top of the walls were enhanced with castellations, the iron roof invisible.

Walking down two wide steps from the entrance hall, where there were grandiose Ali Baba-shaped earthenware pots and an impressive brass jug with a decorative handle and a soft Eastern rug on the floor, and into the inspiring split-level sitting room, the commanding view looked out through three enormous, eight feet wide by six feet high, plate-glass sliding windows.

The sitting room was forty feet by thirty, decorated to perfection with exotic Persian rugs, a sofa set in dove pink and a number of Lamu-style chairs with carved wooden backs. The paintings gracing the stony walls were created by Mother, Andrew, and me. Copper and brass trays from Zanzibar and other ornaments shone as the light caressed them. The lion skin looked very impressive fixed to one wall. Arabian wooden chests with brass ornamentation, built and carved in Lamu and Zanzibar, were part of the tasteful décor.

A small diesel-operated engine and generator provided power for our electric lighting only started up in the evenings. We would sit round the enormous circular fireplace with its inviting log fire after sunset, relaxing with a glass of wine, reading our books, or conversing with one another.

This magnificent and totally unique home was visited by many people from all parts of the world who found its fascination of style and beauty incomparable. From a short distance away and driving towards the fort at night, it looked very much like a floating castle with its many lights twinkling in the darkness—a dream come true.

Years later, in 2003, and a year after Enasoit had sadly been sold, this splendid and noble castle of wonder—our home, which we thought we would live in forever—was completely demolished, right to the very ground from where it had evolved, by the new landowners. And now, a totally different and more modern structure stands in the place of our dream, our beloved castle.

LOOKING AFTER THE STOCK

And at the end of a passing day
When the sun sinks low in the West,
Home you will fly, on winged feet
To perfect peace and rest

—Thelma G. Hall

Milky swathes of salmon-pink clouds dusted the turquoise sky of dawn like a unique painting, gradually changing to a gentle blue, with cream frothy clouds streaking the sky as the sun rose. The silhouette of Mount Kenya dominated the view as we trekked along on foot in the soft sand looking for the tracks of our stolen stock. It was difficult tracing their spoor until reaching slightly harder ground.

We followed the trail for miles. Midday approached, and we finally found their prints mingled with hundreds of others, stock belonging to the Samburu people, the very people who had stolen our steers the day before.

The previous evening, just as we were enjoying our sundowners, there had been a knock at the back door; worried conversation could be heard. Opening the heavy wooden door, the headman, Harun, a dismal look on his dark face, stood outside with one of the herdsmen. Thirty-three head of young cattle were missing. This was the conclusion after the usual evening count by the herdsmen and night guards.

The man said he thought some of his herd went missing on the return to the boma, so he'd gone back a little way towards where they had been grazing during the day and found some strays in the bush. He collected them and brought them back to join the rest, thinking that all was normal, until they counted

17

three times over to make quite sure. And so here we were, trudging along, mile after long and dusty mile, now all trace was lost.

We had no idea which way to turn. There were hundreds of cattle tracks leading in all directions. There was no alternative but to give up the search on foot and head back through the bush and over rough, dry country to the Land Rover and home.

The next move was to get the aircraft out of its hanger, fill it up with fuel, and start the engine. As the propeller eagerly whistled round, we taxied out to the end of the airstrip, took off, and headed north to look for the stock from the air. We saw vast herds of native cattle in that northern Samburu country, but there was no chance of finding ours in the great expanse of northern Kenya on this occasion. This was just one of the many stock thefts we suffered over the years of our long and exciting ranching life.

On other occasions we would sometimes find our stolen stock from the air. Once, as we looked down and searched over the dry semi-desert, a small trail of dust appeared in the distance, streaming out behind dark dots that became larger by the second as we sped towards them. This time, as we flew overhead, we saw a small group of cattle being driven on the hoof at speed through the bush, along game and stock trails.

Turning steeply and diving towards them always put fear and high spirits through my body, and so it did the stock rustlers, who would dash for cover, drop their spears and rungus while tearing through the thorn scrub, in some cases losing their colourful shukas, their ebony naked bodies hiding under bushes, leaving the cattle to scatter as the high-pitched noise of the aircraft screamed over them.

Our pick-up with Harun and stockmen would be heading in the general direction, following the aircraft and watching our movements. We would circle the vehicle, then fly towards the stolen cattle and, yet again, dive over them, feeling our stomachs lifting somewhere towards the ceiling and, as we pulled back to shoot upwards our bodies pressed hard into our seats.

On seeing this, our men would drive to the spot, leap out of the pickup truck and recover the stock, and then walk them back home. Harun would also return with the vehicle. We would circle around in the aircraft, gain a little more height, and head home.

It was dramatic and emotional, stimulating and sometimes electrifying, but never boring. To think of a tranquil existence … well, that would never be while cattle trading. That life was wild and wonderful.

On a few occasions, we and our men managed to capture the tall, elegant Moran-warrior cattle-rustlers, who would then be taken to the nearest police station, sometimes going to jail for a spell. These wild young men, with red shukas worn around their slim waists, coloured beads around their necks and rings of ivory in their ear lobes, their decorative bodies painted with red ochre shining on black skin, long hair finely braided with ochre, were now captured and sitting in the back of the pickup. They were armed with long spears and slim knives that were attached to their waists on leather thongs, and they looked at us with slanting eyes of total despondency at having been caught. I would look back at them, a certain amount of heartfelt pity, even though they had just stolen our livelihood—our precious steers.

I always thought how wonderfully stimulating it must have been for them, setting out with the full intention of raiding stock they'd had their eyes on for months. They would creep up on the unsuspecting herdsman, seizing and tying the poor terrified man to a nearby tree, and then make off across country with prize stock, increasing their own already vast herds.

The warriors know how to communicate with cattle, and they could put them at total ease while stealing them! They would walk our stock for many miles if they managed to get away with them. Sometimes we recovered our stolen beasts two hundred miles or more away from home. I recall once when the herdsmen captured the young thieves and Harun drove them to the police station. As he slowed down to go through the ranch gate, all the warriors jumped out of the back of the truck and ran like the wind! Never to be seen again … well, not for a while. Even the stock thieves who were caught and jailed, never gave up this practise once they were free again—no matter how many times they were caught!

Life on a Kenyan ranch on the borders of the Northern Frontier was wild and extremely exciting. All our stockmen and night guards were armed with shotguns to protect against theft, lions, and hyenas. We also carried guns ourselves on occasion when walking through the bush. As I write this story of my life, things have not changed for a rancher. Stock is still rustled, and lions and other wild animals will still take livestock if they get the chance. This is life in the wilderness: primitive and wild. A life I would not be without.

The cattle were kept in herds of approximately a hundred and fifty head, looked after by one man. Each herd had its own chosen area on the ranch to graze in, and when the grazing got poor, the herd would be moved to another area. Driving long, rutted, dusty, and winding bush tracks, we always used four-wheel drive vehicles: a Suzuki Jeep, Land Rover, or Range Rover to get around the ranch, unless we walked to visit each herd of cattle to check on where they were grazing. It was such a joy walking or driving on warm, sunny days and seeing cobalt skies with puffs of cotton wool clouds. Dust followed our trail as we moved along. Slowing down, the fine powder-like dust would catch up and float through the open windows, covering the inside of the vehicle and ourselves.

The younger stock was put on the sparser grazing areas, leaving the finest areas for the older ones, so they would gain weight and become saleable. The white Boran "Somali Whites" always looked the best of the native stock, putting fat on their backs, particularly the rump and tail areas. Their shapely humps would fill out and they would gleam, their skins giving a soft silky and healthy glow as they wandered in and out of the acacia trees, feeding contentedly. These cattle were from the Kenya-Somali border area and walked, over a period of time, approximately five to six hundred miles. We would purchase them from the auction sales that took place in areas all over the country: Isiolo, Longapito in the north, as far south as MacKinnon Road, and even the coast north of Malindi.

The Northern Frontier stock is almost totally immune to tick-infected diseases, so go through the spray race only once every three months or so. The well-bred Borans bought from neighbouring ranches were not immune, having been sprayed or dipped, from young calf age before we purchased them, in solution to kill the ticks, which attached themselves to the animals' bodies, particularly underneath their tails, where the skin is soft and delicate, inside their ears, and other sensitive parts. So every week to ten days the herds of quality ranch-bred animals would come in from various areas of the ranch to the stockyards to be sprayed. It was always a fine opportunity to count the stock ourselves and go through each animal to check its condition and general health.

On spraying mornings I would wear a long skirt, a simple top, and be adorned with Turkana bead jewellery that our herdsmen's' wives had given me as gifts. The wives would be delighted to see me wearing what they spent hours making for me, gleaming faces of happy smiles, themselves covered from their chins to their breasts in heavy colourful beadwork.

In the hot dry season, we would watch the cattle stream in, usually in single file, dust billowing into clouds around them as they walked purposefully towards the yards. They would all be retained in their own herds, so one herd after another would walk through the spray, then stand in the draining yard for a few minutes, the excess solution dripping off and running into a drain that took it back into the sump to be recycled through the pump and then the spray nozzles onto the next lot of animals. After spraying, the herds would go back to their grazing area.

During the wet season, they would be tramping through thick, stodgy mud, which stuck in their hooves, and the yards area would be a mass of mud mingled with cattle dung, smelly and unpleasant. At times like this, the mud would soon get into the spray nozzles and block them, so the operation would come to a halt while we cleaned out the nozzles and flushed the system through, and then the process would continue. The spraying operation would start at seven in the morning, and, so long as all went to plan, we could get through six to seven hundred head by nine-thirty. Then we would go home to a greatly anticipated and delightful, cooked breakfast.

Once, or sometimes twice a day, the cattle would be taken to drink at the dams, but if the manmade water holes dried out, which would happen in an extremely dry season, they would drink the borehole water from the troughs. Each month, the cattle would be individually weighed to check on their increase in weight gain. The heavier animals would be put into a separate herd to feed on the best grazing, and then finally they would be ready for selling.

The acrid smell of burning grass, the sight of smoke drifting in rolling waves along the valley, and suddenly the entire hillside was alight. With the wind blowing at gale force, sparks would fly and flames would shoot up into trees. The crackling sound of fire would eat up grass, and any small creature unable to get away from the agonizing heat would be consumed by the flames tearing along at a terrifying rate.

Invariably the fires would be triggered off by wandering tribesmen, smoking out bees from a hive within a large acacia tree, to get the much prized and deliciously sweet honey. When a spark taken by the wind caught the tinder dry grass, there would be no stopping the flames, their eager tongues lashing out to devour all in their path.

The operation of trying to beat out the flames as they sped along with branches from the greenest bushes or wet sacks was an extremely exhausting one. Coughing and choking as the smoke filtered into our throats and lungs, the flames licked up the oxygen and left us gasping for air, the tremendous heat soaking all the moisture from our weakening bodies. We would carry water in the vehicle, which would be parked a long way off on a bare area of ground for safety. Weary and covered in soot, clothes torn, we slumped our way back for a much needed long drink after abandoning the fight, severe exhaustion having taken over. The blaze continued to circumnavigate the areas we had just worked on.

Sometimes we would, with all our labour, manage to control and finally put out the fires. Other times it was impossible.

On many occasions, neighbours would see the smoke rising in clouds from a distance and come with all their men to assist in putting out the fires. After a devastating fire, the countryside— every tree, bush, and blade of grass—would be totally burned black and charred, looking like a scene from Hell itself.

The thought of handling guns was quite novel, but the thought of hunting to kill was not something I wanted to think about. Sometimes, however, it is very necessary to hunt for food. It is also necessary to be able to handle a gun for self-protection when living in the wilderness amongst wild animals.

So when I was fourteen years old, my father taught me how to handle both shotguns and rifles. A while later, I had my own 4.10 shotgun, which I carried when walking alone in the bush, and I would shoot guinea fowl and spur fowl for the pot. My mother would make wonderful meals for us; guinea fowl pâté was a favourite. Years later I owned a BSA 12-bore shotgun, and right now a Boita pump-action shotgun.

In difficult times when the weather was very dry and there was very little milk, we needed to hunt either the rich, red-brown impala or the lighter tan-coloured Grant's gazelle with the dark stripe along its belly to substitute the rations for our labour. Maize meal without milk is not very palatable, so a little meat would keep smiles on the faces of our men and their families during harsh times. Sometimes we would shoot one of the spirally twisted, horned eland. These large bovine are splendid leapers when alarmed and will jump high fences if necessary.

I always hated the days when we had to hunt; I felt sadness in my heart for the beautiful creatures, even though there was an abundance of plains game. As we approached, I would always mentally will them to run to safety! On occasions I would do the shooting, but mostly I preferred to let father do it. He resented having to kill just as much as I did, but we needed to feed our people and ourselves at times. If I was doing the shooting, I would use the Winchester 30-30 Saddle Carbine; it was a lighter gun and I could handle it well.

The two of us would lift the days' hunt into the back of the Land Rover pickup. If they were the smaller buck, we would take them out to each boma and drop them off together with other rations: maize meal, sugar, tea, and fat.

The ranch being ten thousand acres, the herds of cattle would be spread out, so we would build bomas made of cut thorn bush from close by, which would be piled up eight to ten feet in a circle surrounding an area of about forty yards round. Inside would be more bush walls to separate each herd. This was where they slept for protection against lions and stock rustlers. There were three or four of these bomas situated around the ranch.

The herdsmen would bring their herds of cattle back to the bomas at about six in the evening and count them in with the night guard who would take over the shotgun of one of the day herders and guard the stock until daybreak, when the day herdsmen would take over their own herds and go out to graze. Most of the cattlemen were of the Turkana tribe. Totally uneducated as far as schooling is concerned, they could neither read nor write but were, and still are as I write, extremely good cattle people and some of the happiest people I have known.

Within the bomas, huts would be built for the men and their families to live in while they were stationed in that particular area. Our men would build the huts of thin poles cut from the bush, with thinner, supple branches woven between the poles, and pack them with mud. In their own homes they would build a mud or grass roof, but we used corrugated iron as it was simple and quick.

As we approached these cattle bomas with rations, medication for stock and people, flies would swarm all over us. The women would come out of their huts covered with coloured beaded necklaces, armlets, and anklets and wearing ragged pieces of material draped around their waists and over their shoulders, which were grey from grime and dust. We would take water in fifty-gallon drums over to them for drinking and washing. The women would occasionally walk down to the waterholes to wash clothes and come back carrying five-gallon containers full of water on their heads, their hips swaying gracefully as they moved slowly along chatting with one another. The children were naked, and flies crawled all over their faces, taking moisture from their eyes, which, strangely enough, didn't seem to bother them at all. The women would be quite content to rub milk or fat into their skin and sit inside the airless huts with a small fire burning, so their clothes and bodies absorbed the smell of smoke. It was the way of life, a tradition which, in their own reservations and on the ranches in the wilderness, still exists today. One would always get the odours of cattle dung and smoke from the cooking fires from over a mile away while heading to their stock bomas.

Soon after moving to Enasoit, the decision was made to try growing ten acres of lucerne next to the main borehole to feed as a supplement to the best of our stock, so they could gain weight faster. We ploughed an area ready for planting, bought light-weight, moveable, irrigation piping and sprinklers, laid the piping on the surface of the ground, and planted the lucerne seed.

Day after day we waited for the seed to germinate, and what an exciting sight when green shoots appeared, pushing their way through the newly ploughed earth. During the dry weather, the borehole was started up on most days. We bought a second-hand, seventy-three horsepower Gardner diesel bus engine from a scrap dealer in Nairobi and hauled the huge piece of equipment home in the back of our Land Rover pickup, which was now almost sitting on its haunches, the front of the bonnet facing somewhere up towards tops of trees! Subsequently, we were stopped by the traffic police. "You don't happen to be overloaded by any chance, Bwana?"

"Oh no, I don't think so. Are we?" Father replied. They insisted most strongly on putting us over the weigh bridge! We were grossly overloaded, of course, and, with a lot of explaining about why we had to get this engine home, the police let us go with a warning.

The Gardner ran the Grundfos turbine, which extracted ten to fifteen thousand gallons of water per hour out of the ground. The clear, mineralised water flowed through a six-inch pipe into a circular, sixty-thousand-gallon concrete-block storage-tank. From the tank, water was pumped through rotating sprinklers onto the growing lucerne, the bright sunlight shining through the showers of water as they spiralled, causing a brilliant rainbow effect.

The lucerne grew incredibly well for the first three years. Fertilizing it every now and again, the lush green area stood out for miles around amid the dry and arid thorn bush, which of course attracted the water buck, eland, zebra, and other plains game, so we were obliged to hire a man to drive away the poor un-favoured animals, who would stand looking longingly at the bright lush green and enticing food.

When the lucerne reached eighteen inches to two feet high, it was usually my job to cut it. I would drive the little red John Deere tractor pulling the Bamford mower behind, knives whizzing back and forth as they sliced through the prolific greenery. The lucerne was then left lying on the ground for a day or two in the hot sun to dry, and then it would be turned over each day. Finally we would pull a sizeable hay rake behind the tractor, collect it all up, and make a haystack.

After a number of years, the ground absorbed a surfeit of high minerals from the borehole water, and the lucerne started to turn yellowish. Each time it was replanted, it grew weaker until eventually we gave up the operation all together, as it had become more work than it was worth.

During the time we used the dry lucerne to feed stock, the men would lay it on the ground in rows and spray it with molasses. The cattle loved it and not only put on weight, but also their coats became shiny. They were extremely healthy animals. I used to rather enjoy driving the little John Deere, being outdoors in the sunshine under clear blue skies, a breeze blowing gently, the smell of newly mown and drying lucerne hay. It was delightful.

I first learnt to drive when I was twelve: Father taught me in a green Morris Minor pickup while we still lived at Nderit Estate. I recall happily driving along a farm road one afternoon when suddenly the steering wheel came away from its moorings. I was left with it in my hands, totally detached from anything! Completely out of control, the car gently veered off to the left, and we ended up in some bushes by the side of the track.

No harm was done, but I was extremely surprised, not expecting such an occurrence.

After moving to Enasoit, I took to driving the old Land Rover and our lovely Wolseley 6/99 mentioned earlier. Finally I took my driving test in October 1967 in a sizeable, left-hand-drive, American Ford Custom. It was a deep metallic-blue, streamlined limousine with chrome bumper bar and headlamp surrounds that we bought from the American Embassy a few years after moving to Enasoit, and after the Wolseley was sold. The exciting automobile looked a little ostentatious zooming along our bush roads, dust streaming out in clouds behind. I loved to drive it, feeling so inspired. The day we bought it, there had been a choice of two cars. The other one was a British make and looked very ordinary to me. I had set my heart on the sleek saloon, my eyes shining with envy at its attractive lines.

***

Boom!

I could not believe my ears or eyes; the sound was like a high-explosive bomb going off. The sixty-thousand-gallon circular water tank was full to the brim, as we had just finished pumping from the borehole. It was there one second and had completely vanished in the next. A most unbelievable sight.

I just stepped off the cattle drinking trough that surrounded the tank, walked fifteen paces, and almost reached the engine shed where Father was coming out through the doorway. I turned round to face the tank, and there, before my eyes, the entire structure and its contents blew up. Seeing it now in slow motion in my mind's eye, the water appeared to rise in the middle of the tank, as every single concrete block in the tank and the trough was blown outwards, flung by the force of sixty thousand gallons of water, thirty or forty yards around from where the tank had stood moments before. We just managed to stumble into the engine shed before the force of the water hit its walls like a tidal wave. Fortunately, the walls remained intact.

What an awful shock and, indeed, a terrifying thought, that we could have been so easily hit by any one of the eighteen-by-six-by-nine-inch concrete blocks being flung through the air. I cannot imagine what would have happened if I still had been standing on the trough wall, or swimming in the tank, as I would so often do when it was first filled. Now, gaping at the open space with not a single block left standing—just a flat expanse of nothing—it was difficult to perceive what had taken place on this otherwise peaceful, sunny day. The luxurious Ford Custom had been parked close to the tank, but miraculously only suffered a free, major, mineralised car wash!

The assumption was that it must have been caused by the corrosive water, having seeped into the blocks and reinforcing over the years, weakening the whole structure. All the large water tanks had been standing for some years before we came to Enasoit. We, of course, rebuilt the tank. Many years later, the very same episode happened again. This time we were not anywhere near it, but discovered no tank when arriving to turn off engine and pump! Needless to say, the next tank we built by that borehole was constructed underground.

Our stockyards, cattle troughs, the spray race, and other buildings were constructed by us and the workers we trained. I learnt to do a lot of cement work and, together with father, built most of the cattle drinking troughs. All those early days on Enasoit I spent outdoors, a wonderful healthy lifestyle. I became gently suntanned, later to be a detriment to my skin! And my short, fair hair turned very blonde.

Way into ranching life, somewhere around the early 1980s, we suffered disaster at the spray race where a dreadful accident took place. Apart from ushering the stock along the crush and into the spray, counting and checking on them, one of the jobs was to clean out the sieve tray every so often. Each time a herd went through, one by one, the dust, dirt, and dung from the cattle would be collected in the sieve, so as not to get into the water in the sump and to protect the nozzles from blocking.

A few days before, we bought a mob of steers from a ranch sixty miles to the west. They had been used to a "plunge dip," where they jump into deep water, swim along approximately an eight-yard channel with anti-tick solution, and climb out the other side to wait patiently in the draining yards.

The new stock walked through the spray race several times without the spray operating, to get them used to a totally different system. Finally, they were walking through with the pump operating at a slow speed with just a light spray coming through. Unbeknown to any of us—as we were all busy doing various jobs—one of the animals jumped and stopped with a shock inside the spray race walls, so the ones following piled up on top of one another until so many were squeezing into the space.

I had cleaned the wooden-framed sieve tray and just shown a young smiley Turkana how to do the job. As I was moving away with my long skirt sweeping across the grass, and he was about to take over the smelly job, the entire wall on our side suddenly came hurtling down and collapsed in a heap around us.

With too many cattle pushing their way through the narrow space, the wall couldn't support the strain put upon it. It missed me by a few inches and two seconds in time. If I had remained where I had been standing—literally a moment before—I would have been completely crushed beneath the wall. The young man was standing slightly to one side of the sieve tray and, unfortunately, part of the wall fell on top of him. It was quite the most horrific situation.

Everybody rushed over to the pitiful scene as cattle scattered in every direction. For a few moments we were totally stunned, and people didn't realize that the poor youth was, in fact, underneath the wall until I yelled out that he was. There was general confusion, and people began to lift the concrete blocks off the part where he had fallen.

The sickening sight appalled us all: the youngster's left leg was severed at the ankle, his foot completely twisted out of the normal position and just hanging on by a thread of skin. He had a gaping hole in the middle of his back, the skin and flesh badly torn away to the backbone, which was protruding through. Blood started to spurt out, oozing down his moist black skin, and then seeped rapidly onto the damp grass. We lifted him gently, but swiftly into the Suzuki Jeep, and Father drove back to the house as fast as possible. I walked back, feeling mortally overcome, very conscious of the fact that he had taken over a job that I had been doing. I felt dazed and very sick.

I could hardly bear to look as we bound his foot back on with heavy bandages and tape. Something had to be done immediately, before Father drove him in the Range Rover at speed to the nearest suitable hospital at the time—two hours' drive to Nyeri. On arrival, we found so many sick people in the hospital needing attention that, for many hours, he was not given the undivided attention that he so badly needed and deserved. He was put in a bed with two other people to start, until a bed just for him was found. During all this, he never uttered a word of complaint. The next steps were drastic: they had to amputate his foot, of course.

Mother, Father, and I went back to Nyeri Government Hospital to visit him often, taking food and some warm clothes. I was horrified to a degree to note that on one occasion his mother, a local "lady of the night," was wearing the very jersey I wore the day we saw him shivering, and I had taken it off to give to him. The hospital only had very thin blankets we discovered. As the weeks passed, things became worse and gangrene set in, so the doctors amputated more of his leg. Finally, they took it off right up to the knee.

Once he recovered enough to leave the hospital, we took him to Nairobi to get him fitted with an artificial leg. He was thrilled and beamed with delight at the prospect. His mother had different ideas and caused us and him endless problems.

He was about eighteen at the time and didn't seem to have a father. The mother forcefully took the artificial leg away from him, saying that she was not prepared to see him with a "false" leg, and compulsively threw it into the back of the Suzuki pickup, all but smashing it. Eventually we bought him crutches and paid for him to have personal training in a number of skills, so he would be able to take jobs that didn't entail moving about too much.

Some years later we saw him in Nanyuki town on his crutches. He had matured and still had as broad a smile as ever.

He also had a job, was well, and very happy with life. He was delighted to have bumped into us.

***

Accidents do happen, particularly in the ranching world. Mother and I were just about to sit down to a simple lunch of brown bread and plum jam, when one of the house staff came in and asked for bandages. A herdsman cut his wrist, the girl reported, so bandages were duly handed out. A few moments later she came back saying, "The bandages are not enough." Very ominous. I looked at Mother questioningly. We both went outside, and there was the herdsman standing on the back porch. His clothing was covered with blood as well as the porch floor where he stood. He had put his spear through his wrist, severing an artery very badly.

When we asked how this happened, he said he was chasing cattle rustlers away from his herd, had stumbled and fallen badly, the spear slicing through his wrist. Together we had an awful job trying to stop the flow of blood, which was pulsating out with each heartbeat, as the troubled man became rapidly weaker. I rushed in for the larger first aid box. Mother cleverly put a tourniquet above his thin, bony elbow, explaining to him that we must release it every few minutes, and then tighten it once more.

We bound his horribly damaged wrist as best we could and were all set to take him to hospital when Harun arrived. He was somewhat shocked at the scene; he'd just heard about the incident and come up to the house from the yards. It was decided that Harun should take him into Nanyuki—an hour's drive away—to the government hospital. The man was actually left with three damaged fingers, although it turned out that he could continue to use his hand almost normally.

After washing down the porch floor with buckets of fresh water, Harun and the herder having left, Mother and I discovered that we weren't feeling particularly enthusiastic about sitting down to our belated bread and plum jam. A large glass of wine was, indeed, very acceptable instead!

31

Each year during the dry season it is always a worry; one never knows whether the rains will come on time or whether there could be a drought. During the years of 1964 and 1965, our area suffered the most horrendous drought: only one and a half inches or rain over a period of eighteen months. Being traders, we managed to sell off some of the stock before things got too desperate. The rest, approximately six hundred head, we moved on the hoof one hundred and twenty five miles to a farm at Solai in the Rift Valley, where they were not experiencing such a bad time. Seven months later, after rain arrived and there was grass again, we walked them all back to Enasoit.

Some of our neighbours lost over a thousand head of stock that died from starvation. One very great friend and neighbour became so depressed that he sold out completely and moved to Voi, three hundred and fifty miles away!

Another really bad drought occurred in 1984. At the time, one of our neighbours who owned a fifty-thousand acre spread, suffered the most horrifying grass fire, something like I described earlier. A man, whose blanket had caught alight inside his hut, threw it outside and, in doing so, set the grass on fire. The wind soon whipped the flames up, and away it went, burning for a week, devastating eighty percent of the unfortunate rancher's land and over three hundred of his sheep. We, and everyone from around the area, went to assist in the operation of trying to get the fire under control. A most exhausting week for us all.

Very soon after this we helped out with grazing for their stock, not realizing just how bad the drought was going to become. Our grazing eventually dwindled, drying up to an inedible consistency. Again, after great difficulty, we managed to sell some of the stock—the reasonably healthy ones. Still, we lost over two hundred head from starvation, forty-five of which were mine.

It was devastating to watch the animals become weaker and weaker. Some just collapsed while drinking at the troughs. We would try and lift them up again, but, too debilitated to stand, their legs would give way and they would just fall yet again. These poor, unfortunate animals would have to be shot to end their miserable days. We tried everything to save them, even cutting bush and covering it with dark rich molasses, but it didn't even save the stronger ones. They just gave up.

The lion, hyena, and leopard were probably amongst the only wildlife that didn't suffer from drought conditions on ranches. Every steer or heifer that died from the drought or had to be shot was towed away from the boma or drinking troughs, where it suffered its last miserable hours. The dead animals would be tied by a rear leg with a rope attached to the back of the vehicle and towed to an open area, where they could be seen by birds of prey and predators. Even the vultures get to be over-fed in these circumstances, which would be happening on every ranch in the area. Eventually, an open graveyard was created on the property with stock carcasses.

Lions would take what little meat there was from the carcasses. Vultures from miles around kept their eyes on the situation and, as soon as they spotted another dead animal, would circle round, dive with wings folded back, make a jet-like sound as they came down at full speed, and then level out just before gracefully landing near the carcase and prancing their way to the meat, where upon they would bury their heads deep into the mortal remains and proceed to squabble over choice pieces.

There were always the Ruppell's griffon with spotted backs, the huge and heavy-billed lappet-faced and the white-backed vultures, and occasionally the smaller and slender-billed Egyptian vulture. Hyenas would come later, chew away at the tough hide, and crunch up the bones. Eventually, everywhere would be left clean with just a bare patch of ground where the vultures had all been scrabbling about, and the odd bone here and there left to be bleached by the scorching equatorial sun.

These were the very worst of times: depressing and desperate. The first of the wildlife to start suffering are the warthogs, whose skins begin to sag and look all wrinkly. The little ones, skinny from lack of milk, try to run, but their small delicate bodies tumble over in their weakness. Then the buffalo begin to decline and finally the rest of the plains game. All the wildlife stand looking dull eyed and dejected with little energy. They barely move out of the way as one drives, or even walks by at times like these.

The boreholes were pumped constantly throughout the dry seasons. Dams would be drying up, leaving little pools of muddy water behind, and sometimes cattle or wildlife would go down to try to drink and horrifyingly get hopelessly stuck in the muddy bottom, too feeble to pull themselves free. Even the tall giraffe can suffer this way, their long legs sinking into the oozing mud and very little strength left to ease them out. It is almost impossible to do anything about this—one cannot get close enough because of the muddy surrounds—but over the years we have managed to save both stock and wild animals on various occasions by walking into the gluey mud, tying a rope around the poor animal, and "towing" it out with the vehicle. Wild animals always caused the greatest difficulty, as it was extremely dangerous trying to undo the rope once they were free from the mud.

Even on the days that we drove to town for shopping, it could be very unpleasant seeing dead cattle lying by the road-side every few hundred yards. They would drop from weak-ness and fatigue after being moved from one place to another in search of better grazing. The stench of dead stock would become unbearable, as the predators and vultures couldn't cope with the amount of "free" meat lying everywhere in drought conditions.

One very dry season, a particular herd of about sixty-five buffalo used to come and drink at one of the cattle troughs. Get-ting so used to seeing us in the Range Rover, they would come bounding towards us like a herd of cattle as we approached. They would stop and wait, tails swishing over their backs to keep flies away, and hold their heads high, sniffing the air as we turned on the tap that let the water come gushing into the trough. Then they would edge closer, make loud sniffing noises, and start to drink. Never mind that we were standing at the same trough! They associated us and the vehicle with watering time, and became very tame.

In yet another drought year, the stock on the far side of Ena-soit was forced to water at the Nanyuki River on the next property. All the dams had dried up on that side. They would only go to water every second day because of the great distances, and then have a full day's grazing on the in-between day.

A herd of elephants would peacefully drink at the river, the babies playing with each other and sliding their way down the muddy riverbank, some standing in the middle of the gently flowing river spraying the cool water over their backs. Our thirsty stock advanced at speed down to the water's edge to drink. Suddenly, seeing the elephants, the cattle became overly nervous and stampeded. One cow elephant worried for her baby and charged. Screaming wildly at the stock as her trunk swayed from side to side spewing water everywhere, she tossed two of our young steers into the river. Being badly damaged by her powerful blows, they both drowned.

TRADING DAYS AND THE CHARACTERS

Selling one and buying two
This is what we'd always do
Selling two and buying four
"Traders" knocking on my door!

—Susan M. Hall

The last quarter of the moon was shining, surrounded by clusters of bright, twinkling stars in the cool, damp air at four in the morning. Father and I and a number of our cattle-men clambered sleepily into the vehicle to make our way to Nanyuki. It became colder and colder, and by the time we reached the bleak railway station to load our stock to go off to the Kenya Meat Commission, we were shivering in the bitter cold air descending from the clear and snowy peaks of Mount Kenya.

Cattle standing in the station yards, their coats all starry from cold, looked around nervously. The herdsmen who walked them from home the previous day huddled together in their overcoats trying to keep warm around a small wood fire, some of them standing with hunched shoulders, hands in their coat pockets.

Out of the gloom the monstrous engine loomed, belching smoke and steam as it warmed up. The couplings clanked and clattered as the engine driver began to manoeuvre trucks into position, ready for loading.

This was just one of many times that we went to load stock at the railway station. On this particular occasion, the engine driver invited Father and me to join him in his cab as he shunted up and down the line. The warmth inside the cab was so wel-come, and we were loath to have to leave it to go and load stock.

Then, over the lower slopes of the misty mountain, a gentle orange glow appeared. The huge orb of the morning sun rose rapidly, and we started to feel the pleasure of warmth soaking through our bush coats as the cattle began to stir. Trucks in position, the men opened the big, heavy doors, which formed a ramp, and our cattlemen scattered the dry hay that we'd brought the day before onto the truck floors.

We began ushering the cattle into the pens and, one by one, loaded them into the trucks, around sixteen head to a bogie. The ramps were all ridged so as not to be slippery, but, as the animals walked up, a certain amount of manure was deposited, so it became slippery, and they stumbled and slid their way in, pushing and shoving one another until the last one's plump back end, still protruding, was given a final push. The doors quickly closed with a crash before the cattle tried to turn round and come out, and huge bolts snapped into position. After the last truck was loaded, the engine driver moved all of them to another line to await the main-line engine, which would take them on to Nairobi.

The loading completed, we filled in the appropriate forms in the stationmaster's office, after which we made our way to The Marina, the little café in town, and ordered hot coffee and tea, and sat sipping the most welcome beverages with the steam rising in front of our cool faces. We would often meet friends there who also were sending their stock off on the same train. Then it was off for home for a late breakfast of crispy bacon, fried bread, and eggs topped with mashed tomatoes.

Cattle auctions were held all over the country, and we would fly to most of them, even the ones at McKinnon Road, which was a long way from home. On one particular occasion, we had flown down and spent almost a week with our good friends— Ray and his wife, Helen—who owned the best part of eighty thousand acres about twenty miles from Voi, a two-hour flight in the Navion from Enasoit. It was May 1968, and the Livestock Marketing Division (L.M.D) was holding a sale with a large number of stock—in the region of six thousand head—and of great interest to ranchers and traders like ourselves.

It was a very short flight, about ten minutes in the Navion from Ray's airstrip near their house to the McKinnon Road airstrip. The L.M.D holding ground for stock where they held the auctions was right by the airfield and just over the road from the railway station, so very convenient for us. Some of the buyers would fly in; others would come by car. It was a long journey for most, at least a full day's drive.

The cattle sold on these auctions were always Northern Frontier Boran stock, cattle bred by various tribes in the dry regions of the country, some having crossed the borders from Somalia and Ethiopia and bought in by the L.M.D. to sell at the auctions to people like us. Being traders of stock, rather than breeders, we would usually purchase a larger number of stock than the ranchers.

The auctioneer, a New Zealander, arrived by car. He was tall and about fifty-five with thinning grey hair. He had a pleasant smile, his teeth a little brown from continuous smoking, and he was extremely good at his job. His long, baggy trousers would blow and flap in the wind as he stood on the wooden platform erected from poles, overlooking the yards, as dust swirled about everywhere from the movement of cattle. Around a hundred and fifty head would be on view, and ready for auction.

Each mob that came into the ring would be marked on the rump by different colour paint. Ranchers started bidding, and each lot would, obviously, work out at a slightly different price. All the cattle were on view outside the yards in mobs of four to five hundred, each mob more or less one colour—one lot white, another brindled, then brown, black, and so on. You would bid for the ones in the ring and, if you got them, you could either take the whole mob from that lot at the price per head that you'd got them for or let someone else take them. If you were a smart trader, you would take the lot—all five hundred—and if you didn't want them all, you'd sell what you didn't want at a profit to someone else before leaving the sale.

We seemed to be bidding against a rather short man, plump around the middle, who wore his shorts very wide, making his exceptionally slim legs appear even thinner. He wore a large felt hat pulled low over his forehead and a pair of dark sunglasses. I couldn't tell where or in which direction he was looking, but he was bidding furiously, determined to get the sleek white mob that we had set our minds on! We actually outbid him on this lot and, at the end of the day, purchased four hundred and fifty head, at an average price of two hundred and sixty-five shillings per head!

Over the years, the price of stock increased tremendously, of course. In early times, we made very good profits on trading, but, as the years passed, the profits became less and less. Finally, by the time Enasoit was sold in 2002, there was little if any profit in cattle trading. During our beef-trading years, I seemed to be the only female trader in beef cattle in Kenya. If there was another, I was never fortunate enough to come across her. I lived in a man's world and enjoyed every moment of the life to the fullest.

One or two wives would join their suntanned husbands to the auctions, but it was usually all men. One young and very attractive fellow with wavy blond hair would always fly in to the sales in a small green and white, high-winged four-seater. He always wore well-fitted shorts and check shirts; he even had an Australian-style Stetson. With a broad smile showing even, white teeth, he was always extremely gracious to me, and I would look forward to seeing his well-formed figure standing there, tanned arms resting on the stockyard rails, looking smilingly at stock he would be interested in. Another gentleman who would always be at every auction would wear neat slacks, a long-sleeved shirt, and a smart little waistcoat in which he would stand with thumbs tucked firmly high it its pockets. He would be topped in a greenish woollen trilby.

The "Baggy Shorts Brigade" always amused me no end, particularly when they wore heavy socks and what appeared to be oversized boots, their knobbly knees showing just below the shorts. There were a number of this style of male, mostly with overly large bellies overhanging their varied leather belts. Some had dark curly hair, some thin fair hair, and some were balding.

Most wore a variation of old, floppy felt hats, greasy and dusty from years of wear. I used to love chatting with them all. They were all so charming.

Around mid-morning they would start to get fidgety and look longingly at their bottles of Tusker lager, which they brought with them in cool bags. Searching deep into their shorts' pockets for a bottle opener, they would pop the cap, and then the tip of the bottle would be put straight between parched, dust-covered lips. They sucked thirstily and satisfyingly on their bottles, like babies suckling hungrily on their milk bottles, their eyes sparkling in faces that were starting to turn red from the morning's scorching sun. The joy and pleasure of the cool liquid showed as it trickled down dry throats. Everybody took picnic-type food, and most of us took beer to quench our thirst throughout the hot, dusty day.

A couple, friends of ours who came to the sales only occasionally, mainly for the interest of seeing the stock, were most decorative. He would arrive wearing slim-style slacks, a long-sleeved shirt, a sleeveless safari jacket, and a lightweight straw Panama hat. His wife would be elegantly clad in a deep-green safari trouser suit, a coloured scarf tied lightly around her neck, and a straw sun-hat adorned with peacock and other feathers that swayed provocatively back and forth each time she moved her head, her pretty, light-strawberry curls escaping beneath the hat. The most stock they ever bought would be twenty-five head, and these usually walked home with whatever stock we bought.

Father dressed in simple khaki slacks and a safari shirt. He never wore a hat, so his fair hair was bleached to a golden blond. His slim, rangy figure was admired by all. I usually wore a Western-style check shirt; my favourite was a soft, pale-green and brown with gold thread running between the large checks. I also wore just-above-the-knee leather-fringed skirts, high leather boots, and an American Stetson hat to protect me from the hot sun. I did seem to cause a stir here and there—eyes followed me up and down the sale grounds, but even with my extreme shyness I still secretly enjoyed being admired! I was always rather conscious of my very skinny figure compared to other young women, who seemed to be attractively curvaceous.

The day after the McKinnon Road sale, we loaded the four hundred and fifty head into cattle trucks at the station and flew home, so as to be at Nanyuki Station to meet them three days later, a three hundred and fifty mile train journey. As it turned out, we were at Nanyuki on the day the train was expected to arrive, but it didn't turn up. It was a very worrying situation, so we got hold of the stationmaster, who contacted various stations along the way, only to discover that the train was delayed for two more days.

We learned later that the engine driver stopped the train at Sultan Hamud to get off to visit a friend, leaving the trucks on the line. Meanwhile, all the cattle were parked in the scorching heat. He didn't appear to feel any responsibility what so ever! Cattle could cope with a three-day journey without water or food with the breeze blowing through the trucks; but it got far too hot for them if the train stopped, which it should never have done!

Five days later, the train finally chugged its way into Nanyuki Station. Desperately upset over this situation, we were feeling extremely apprehensive as to what we would find on opening the truck doors, as the stench coming from the whole train was quite considerable as it approached.

Gaunt and weary from their dreadful trauma, their ribs pro-truding through their flesh, eyes wide, glassy and terribly tired, some of the cattle stumbled out. Others fell out and some still lying down in the trucks had to be lifted out. The poor animals could hardly walk, cramped from the extended days' journey. Several had acquired broken legs and had to be transported home in the back of the pickup.

The unperturbed driver got out from the train, smiling as if nothing untoward had taken place. In situations as this one, or indeed any other of this nature, the rancher or trader is not compensated for loss or damage in Kenya, and we have to bear the total brunt of the outcome ourselves. Financial losses were often great.

41

There was water laid on for the stock, and they drank long-ingly and thirstily from the troughs in the station compound, and then they started little by little to munch into the grass around and about. We brought hay for the ones that couldn't stand, and, after two days' rest in the station grounds, our men slowly walked them twenty-five miles back home. A week later they were unrecognisable, still very thin, but healthy and happy, having been out grazing each day and enjoying the borehole water.

Another drastic incident on the rail in the mid-1960s occurred on a cattle train bound for Athi River to the Kenya Meat Commission from Nanyuki. The train was loaded up with fat stock: some belonging to us, and the rest from three or four other ranches. During these times, some of the new engine drivers were not experienced. They had not undergone the full training that a professional railway engine driver should have had, and so there were a number of very nasty and unfortunate accidents.

On this bright, sunny morning, an hour or so after we loaded our fat stock, the train was hurtling along at full speed, the wagons swaying, their metal wheels singing along the line, while the cattle were becoming very unstable inside. Suddenly, one truck slipped out of control, sparks flying from its wheels, screeching on the rails. The weight and speed being beyond what the truck could endure, it left the track, dragging five or six other bogies off the line with it.

As the wagons came flying off the line at high speed, doors burst open and cattle were flung out into the air. Some were crushed to death by the heavy trucks as they crashed, sliding their way along the ground. Cattle were mortally wounded, suffering broken backs and legs, and injured internally. Some, not so badly damaged, managed to stumble to their feet and limp into the grass totally stunned and bewildered.

We received the horrifying message later that day. On reaching the scene of the derailed train, the sight was absolutely horrendous. Dead and dying cattle were lying by the side of the railway line, while others were scattered around, looking so pathetic and lost. We were forced to shoot our wounded animals, as there was no way of saving them. The ones that could still walk were collected up, and our herdsmen walked them slowly back fifteen miles to Nanyuki, and then, eventually, back to Enasoit.

After the Kenya Railways ceased to operate for stock transportation, some owners of lorries took over. At one time we were selling a lot of cattle to a company called Delmonte, which had a pineapple canning factory at Thika, twenty miles out of Nairobi, and a large area of pineapple plantations. At the time I am writing about, they also had a feedlot for beef animals. They would buy stock, put them in sizable pens, and feed them on ground-up pineapple waste mixed with molasses to fatten them for sale.

Over a period of time, we sold hundreds of head of our best quality cattle to them. An exceptionally gracious man, who was tall, rather heavy, with a gentle and kind personality, had five lovely daughters who used to come out with him when he did the buying for the company, and it could work out that sometimes we would weigh over the scales four or five hundred head in a day.

In previous years, everybody bought and sold by eye—estimating the weight and value of the animals—which was a lot of fun, because it required all the skill one had. Ranchers and traders would often ask me for my advice on the value of stock. I would guess the weights of cattle and, invariably, would be four of five kilograms out in possibly a four hundred and fifty-kilogram animal! But, by the 1970s, many of the ranches had cattle-weighing scales, so each animal was bought or sold at so much per kilogram. We still bought and sold by eye when the opportunity arose.

After selling steers to Delmonte on one occasion, the lorries all arrived. Five of them in various colours backed up, one at a time, to our loading ramp. Usually, around eighteen head were loaded onto the Mercedes lorry. As with the railway trucks, we always scattered hay on the floors to make it more comfortable for the cattle. Having loaded all five vehicles, they left, one by one, with friendly waves coming from the smiling drivers as they slowly moved off along the murram road, a dust trail left behind wafting high into the air.

43

Not having a telephone in our home, because of living so far away from civilisation, we would have to drive the twenty-five mile journey into Nanyuki to be able to communicate with anyone. So we drove in to phone Delmonte the following day to make sure that all the cattle had arrived safely at their destination. We were told that only four of the Mercedes lorries had arrived!

One lorry suffered major problems with the cattle. Several animals had lain down on the floor and others trampled on top of them, causing great turmoil in the back of the lorry. The poor distressed driver had no alternative but to stop on the side of the road, and, with his turn-boy, tried to get the downed animals to stand back up again, but failed. Eventually, they were compelled to open the back doors to try and let some of the harassed cattle out, but, of course, they *all* pushed their way out.

This incident took place in the lush, green farmland area of Karatina, where rivers and trickling streams flow gently through the valleys surrounded by Kikuyu farms. Unfortunately, two animals were suffering while the chaos took place. The turn-boy who was keeping watch on the situation had done his best, but the stock became restless and got completely out of control. Now sixteen head were out and wandering about on the main tarmac road and likely to get run into by other cars. Some strayed into a Kikuyu farmer's compounds and started chewing on his well-formed maize plantation. Seeing this, he came out, perturbed at losing some of his crop, collected all the rest up, and very kindly put them into a pen by his house.

After receiving this news, Father arrived on the scene, set on thanking the kind man for his most appreciated assistance. Father was given huge bunches of beautiful, yellow-skinned bananas from the farmer's plantation. Father and our men now had to dig into the bank on the roadside to make a place for the lorry to reverse up against and reload the sixteen head, having deposited the two dead steers on the man's land. He was delighted—no doubt he and his neighbours would enjoy *nyama choma* (roasted meat over charcoal) for weeks to come.

***

Father used to frequently fly the L.M.D. manager up to northern Kenya to do the buying of stock for the auctions. It would sometimes work out that Father and our friend, Ray, would also buy at the same time as the L.M.D., and so all the stock would walk the five or six hundred miles south, with armed guards provided by the L.M.D. in an attempt to protect them from cattle raiders, mainly Somalis, in that area.

In those days, the general populace was not allowed to venture into those north-eastern regions of wilderness without special permission, which, of course, my father and the L.M.D. had. Women certainly were not permitted to enter those areas, so I only flew up there once or twice with Father. Somalia was continuously invading north-eastern Kenya—they wanted those northern territories of the country and were raiding African villages and homesteads belonging to the Boran and other tribes, quite apart from their own people living in north-eastern Kenya. The Somalis stole their stock and killed people, even stealing their women. Almost any vehicle that drove up there was ambushed, the people shot and all their belongings stolen, which made the situation for buying cattle in the area very difficult, but this was where they were available.

The Somalis were even setting mines in the roads as far south as Nanyuki. There are many Somali people living in Kenya who have transport and trading businesses, and even these unfortunate traders had their own trucks blown up! We would witness the terrible destruction caused by the road mines when lorries were towed into Nanyuki. The wrecks were unrecognizable: their seats ripped and stained with blood from the poor, ill-fortuned driver and whoever else happened to be in the lorries.

On one memorable occasion, we were landing at Marsabit in the North, not far from the Ethiopian Border, and, as we touched down on the airfield, open Land Rovers laden with armed men in army uniforms approached us at high speed and drove parallel on either side of us as we sped along keeping up. All guns trained on us, the urge to take off again was considerable, but they were just too close, and had we done so there is no doubt that they would have riddled our aircraft with bullets. They were the local army and weren't expecting a plane to land that day, although a report had been sent. They had no idea who we were, even though we couldn't have looked like Somali invaders. They were obviously a little trigger happy, but on the alert due to current circumstances. It was somewhat unnerving to say the least!

***

On one favourable opportunity, Father and Ray flew up north to buy stock together with the L.M.D. They eventually purchased three thousand six hundred and forty head after hours of haggling. Around six hundred head of these were to be shared between ourselves and Ray. According to rule, the L.M.D. hired armed scouts to bring the stock south on the hoof. During the long walk of over five hundred miles, Father would fly the L.M.D. manager north several times a week to keep an eye on the movements of all the cattle heading south.

It so happened that on this flight out to look for the livestock, Father, Ray, and Doug were unable to locate them. They flew all over the north-eastern area where the cattle were expected to be trekking, but there was no sign of a dust trail anywhere. They flew along the dry river courses, around hills and mountains, searching endlessly, but there was no sign. Losing thousands of head seemed quite out of the question. The men flew back home, ultimately worried and considered what to do next. Mother gave lunch to everyone, and we all sat discussing the situation. Finally, Father refuelled the aircraft and they flew off once again.

Circling around now at high altitude over lava country east of Mount Kenya, they spotted a crater where there looked to be cattle milling about in the bottom. Losing height rapidly, they flew over to have a closer look. Most certainly these were cattle, and, on flying down into the crater, they discovered that they were indeed the very ones they were searching for!

It was always a fair possibility that the scouts employed to bring the cattle back would be involved with the stock raiders.

We were so used to losing around ten percent of the cattle coming across the miles and miles of desolate and rough country with theft and deaths, but we hadn't expected to lose the lot! They obviously had planned it out well and hidden all the cattle in this crater hoping not to be discovered—all three thousand six hundred and forty head. What an enormous achievement for those scouts! Had Father and his friends not located them, it would have been a disastrous loss for us and the L.M.D., if they had got away with it. Later, there were some wild and wonderful excuses for the fact that the stock were in the crater.

Inside craters there are always tremendous downdrafts. Father and friends in the Bonanza flying round hit one and were sucked down, losing height at the rate of one thousand feet per minute. Doug hit his head on the aircraft roof and, being bald, suffered a nasty cut. It was a very unpleasant experience for them all when the plane descended downward. Fortunately, the Bonanza was a powerful aircraft, but even with full throttle they had a struggle pulling out of this most vicious downdraft. Finally, they pulled up and out of the crater.

Needless to say, five days later, the exhausted herd of cattle reached their destination. We split the six hundred Somali whites with Ray. If I remember correctly, I took sixty of these thin, but good quality steers. The three thousand and forty were put up for auction three months later. All stock coming in from the north is compelled to be put into quarantine for a time on the L.M.D. holding grounds and inoculated for various diseases, so as not to pass any unsuspecting sickness on to any of the home-bred cattle on the ranches.

Many of the auction sales were held at Longapito, sixty miles north of Enasoit. We would usually fly there as it was far quicker—the road was, and still is, extremely rough, with rocky outcrops and sandy river beds to cross and areas washed away in the previous rainy seasons. The scenery is magnificent with pale-blue mountains—the Mathews Range in the distance, rising out of the heat haze, its nine-thousand-foot peaks caressed by little puffs of white clouds gently dispersing as fast as they form—and an open savannah interspersed with acacia trees. It was a very convenient area for us to buy from, as it took only about four days to walk cattle home.

As with the McKinnon Road auction, which was over four hundred miles away, all the same people came to the Longapito sales, and a few more besides. There were a number of Rumuruti ranchers who came on occasion. One very tall, slim man with fair curly hair, long khaki slacks and a faded blue-check shirt flew low over the sale, landed, had a quick look round at all the stock, turned round, walked swiftly back to his aircraft, and flew off again. Obviously on his way to somewhere else.

The manager of another ranch from the same area came chugging along in a tatty, old, short-wheelbase Land Rover. The paint peeling off in places and smoke belching out of its exhaust, it sounded like a worn out tractor. An exceptionally shy Danish man by the name of Hans, who we had known since I was a small girl of five when we lived in the Wanjohi Valley in the early fifties, modestly stepped out, blinking as he turned to look at all the other people, his fair, straight hair with a side parting neatly combed. His clothes always looked a size too big for him: long, loose trousers that hung well over his highly polished shoes and bagged at the knees and sleeves of his jackets hanging halfway down his hands. He would have half a cigarette hanging from his lips, and then his shy smile would reveal his tobacco-stained teeth.

At the end of the sale, we bought three hundred and sixty-five head and organised some men from the area to bring them as far as the Northern Frontier District Border barrier, about eight miles north of Enasoit. Two armed L.M.D. scouts would always accompany them. Our own herdsmen would meet them at the barrier and bring them home. We would drive out to the incoming stock with rations for the men: loaves of bread, tins of corned beef or any kind of tinned meat and milk. This would satisfy their hunger on these long treks. They relished the meat rations, which they wouldn't benefit from very often on an average working day on the ranch, unless we had shot a buck or two for them. The tired and dust-covered herders always had broad smiles on their faces when we arrived with rations. They enjoyed the cattle-trekking trips; it was something different from their every day lives, and friends would often be met along the trail.

The Kirimon sale ground was only about forty miles, as the crow flies, from the Longapito one, but cattle would walk a different route back. Kirimon area is west of the Ewaso Nyiro River and up on the escarpment, so it was simpler to bring the stock along the top country. They would have to cross the Ewaso Nyiro and Nanyuki Rivers to get to Enasoit, which meant trekking through a number of other people's ranches, so we would always get permission from them first. They were mostly very pleasant and amicable people, so there was little if any trouble bringing our cattle through.

I remember one time in particular when we had purchased around three hundred head from a Kirimon auction. In the Aberdare Mountains, there had been heavy rain, which had come gushing down, and the Ewaso Nyiro River was pounding along and overflowing its grassy and acacia-grove banks. The cattle and herders were held up for a day and a half, camping close by, while we waited for the river to abate.

Even as we waited there was yet more rain, and it was decided that the stock should cross before the next burst of water came down. It was an arduous job getting the first of the cattle to move close enough to jump into the swirling, muddy-brown water of the Ewaso Nyiro River. The men were whooping and whistling, trying desperately to encourage the very wary animals to swim across. The roaring and gurgling sound of the river as it gushed and rolled its way past was quite unnerving. The stock kept trying to turn back. With the men's insistence, the first cattle finally took a flying leap into the turbulent river, and then the rest followed, one after another. They were carried downstream as they fought the strong current to reach the far bank. The sight was spellbinding and dramatic: an arc of cattle swimming across with the water whirling over their backs. The first ones arrived and clambered lethargically up the muddy banks. The followers realised that all was well, and the stragglers went in with little concern.

***

The heavens opened, and the Dol-Dol road was frighteningly slippery and thick with mud. Mother, Father, Andrew, and I were all in the front of the Land Rover pickup, which was very heavily loaded with a second-hand plough, bought from a farm sale of stock and implements. We were on our way home, travelling slowly. All our shopping was squeezed in the cab with us, including a tray of eggs perched precariously on Andrew's knees.

Rivers of water were flowing along the sides of the road, the ditches overflowing. The windscreen wipers operated on their one and only speed, but the heavy rain outdid the wiping, so it was laborious trying to see out. Intense lightning flashed before our tired eyes and claps of loud thunder exploded in our ears. The road was becoming a quagmire of slush.

Approaching a culvert, the road narrowed considerably, and the watercourse was full of swirling, muddy water. Instantly the Land Rover started to slide sideways, the weight of the plough creating momentum. There was no way that we were going to remain on this sticky thoroughfare. We watched the culvert getting nearer as the wheels slipped towards it, even though the brakes were fully on. We just kept on sliding into the running water of the enormous drain.

It was a critical situation and there was no way of getting out of this position. Water started seeping into the cab. We had fallen on top of one another. Father opened his door, and we cascaded out, one at a time, into a stream of chocolate-coloured liquid, Andrew still clutching the tray of eggs intact! Mother, Andrew and I stood by the roadside in the deluge for two hours, cold, soaked, and thoroughly miserable, while Father trudged all the way home, across country to get assistance.

***

At one time during the 1960s, I owned a beautiful fat-tailed, black-faced Persian ram that was herded together with a small flock of ewes we had. I was proud of him and had owned him from birth. One cool, starry night, I heard the sheep making faint bleating sounds. Not thinking too much about it, I turned over and snuggled under my duvet.

The following morning we received a report from the young shepherd that my ram was missing, later to be discovered that he had been stolen by Samburu raiders and slaughtered behind the aircraft hangar, only fifty yards from the sheep boma. We followed their trail way up over the top of the Lolldaiga Hills. There was nothing to be done; they would enjoy this mutton. My sweet ram was dead, and I was very upset about it. He had been more of a pet than anything else.

The karakul is an Asian breed of sheep. Most unfortunately and very, very sadly, they are slaughtered a few days after birth for their beautiful, silky soft and black curly fleeces. It so happened that our friend Ray had a flock of karakuls, not for the purpose mentioned, but he just enjoyed breeding them and seeing them on his property. I told Ray one morning, when we were over at their place, about my poor black-faced Persian ram being stolen, whereupon he sent his headman out to the flock to bring in a karakul lamb to give to me as a present! He was the most adorable little creature, and I took him home in my arms. He grew into the most magnificent ram, the only black one in our flock. He had thick, curly black wool.

One windy afternoon, whirlwinds blowing dust into the warm air, Ray arrived. "Sue, do you think I could buy that karakul ram back from you?" he asked.

"Oh, why Ray?" I replied.

"Well, you see, the wretched Somalis stole all my rams last night, and so I've only got ewes left!" he laughed heartily.

"Ray, I will give the ram back to you," I told him. "After all, you gave him to me in the first place!"

Ray wouldn't entertain the idea, however, and he offered me two hundred shillings, which was a good price at the time, and away went my karakul ram.

Over all our trading years, butchers from around the country came to Enasoit to buy cattle. They would always choose the really fat cows or heifers in preference to steers. The female stock put more fat on their rumps, and most people in Africa have a tendency to eat meat with a coating of fat attached, which is much more succulent, tender, and tasty.

Our stock was supplied to Nairobi hotels, restaurants, and safari lodges all over the country. There is a company by the name of Farmer's Choice that would buy large numbers of our cattle—their products are distributed countrywide to supermarkets, hotels, clubs, and small shops. Even as I write, they pack their meat products beautifully, and I often watch housewives popping the neat little packages into their trolleys as they whizz around the supermarkets. Of course, I do the same thing myself when shopping day comes around about every ten days.

On rare occasion, we would sell our young stock to other traders or ranchers to fatten the cattle instead of keeping them ourselves. Sometimes more profit could be made by keeping the cattle for only two or three months. At such times, we would sell them by eye, putting a value on them, and then the buyer would either take them at our price or we would come to some other agreement. We seldom had a problem selling.

A fleet of enormous Leyland Hippo lorries arrived. We could see them from our home as they approached the loading ramp three miles away. The lorries would accommodate thirty head or more of large animals. These trucks belonged to a company that was buying stock for export to Oman and Saudi Arabia. Over a period of time, we sold thousands of head to this trading agency. The giant lorries would take the cattle all the way to Mombasa, a four hundred and fifty mile journey. From the trucks they would be loaded into ships that would take them through the warm, blue waters of the Indian Ocean.

The ships were fitted out extremely well for cattle, which we had made sure of before we would sell our stock. Shade, food, and water were all arranged for the journey. The buyers could not afford to let stock lose weight or come to any harm. They had to make sure that they would make their profit too.

***

Flying to other peoples' ranches was always tremendously exciting. Not only was I interested in their stock, but the people themselves were such a variation of interesting characters. Everyone had a different style of home: some were luxurious in their décor, with the family silver very much in evidence. The Earl Grey tea would be served in beautiful bone-china cups, with a gentle floral design. After weighing cattle all morning, one felt far too dusty and dirty to dare sit in the damask-covered easy chairs.

Other homes were quite different. There would be lovely old wooden tables covered with medication for stock and veterinary books, muster rolls, and sadly neglected broken chairs and sofas—their springs having collapsed—with covers torn from many years of wear. Cushions with the remains of a European design would be faded to pale colour, and fraying curtains, once rich with embossed patterns, would hang beside small windows overgrown with creepers and were down in places where curtain rings were missing. Dogs and puppies would sit on almost every chair, while cats sharpened their claws on worn rugs. Everyone would be welcoming and more than hospitable.

Since childhood I have been interested in interiors and design, so I always enjoyed seeing peoples' ranch houses, no matter what style. On cattle expeditions, we would arrive at seven in the morning and enjoy a variety of different breakfasts and a good chat with the host and hostess before going off to weigh the stock. If we were weighing five or six hundred head, we would still be there for a very late lunch and a chance to chat about subjects other than cattle before flying home. They were long and exhausting days but enjoyable and rewarding.

All cattle on ranches are inoculated against foot-and-mouth disease every six months by the veterinary department. Not that the sickness really affected the local native stock to any great degree, but it is compulsory. It keeps the animals free of it so they can be sold at any time, otherwise, the ranch could be in quarantine for some while and business held up.

THE RAINY SEASON

The distant hills are misty with rain;
Falling at last on the vast African plain.
The parched and arid earth will be
Returned to its beauty and glory again.

—Thelma Hall

When heavy drops of rain hit and bounce on the dry, hard ground, little puffs of dust are blown up, until finally the parched earth thirstily drinks in each droplet of rain as it begins to pour down. As the damp soaks in, the pungent and delightful scent comes wafting through the half-open windows. Bolts of lightning strike so brightly for an instant against the deep, dark purple of angry sky, and then the crashing sound of thunder comes moments later. The first rain of the season is, without any shadow of doubt, a tremendous joy to wildlife, domestic stock, and people.

I stood watching with awe the dark, rolling blue-grey clouds grazing their way along the hills and into the valleys. Little rivulets of water trickled down the panes as the storm hit our corrugated iron roof with force. The noise was quite deafening.

When a really heavy storm produces two inches of rain in a short period of time in the area of the hills, the water flows rapidly, forming gushing rivers along the gullies, and it pours into the dams, filling them with millions of gallons of water in a matter of half an hour. If the rain continues, the dams are in danger of bursting. With too much water flowing in at one time, the overflows cannot always cope with the inflow, so the water builds up and starts to flow over the top of the earth walls, eating into them. This happened on a number of memorable occasions after very heavy storms.

Reddish-brown coloured water was flowing into the earth dam at the bottom of our airstrip with tremendous force, carrying silt from the hills along with it. We were watching with trepidation from the Range Rover as the water rose towards the top of the wide earth-wall. Father and I walked along the wall and started to furiously shovel soil from the back, onto the top, and in the middle, in the faint hope that it would make the wall just a little bit higher and stop the water from trickling over the top. But it rained again in the hills, and a new flood arrived.

Standing on the wall watching, we saw water start to trickle over the top. In no time, it was cutting a channel, flowing faster and faster as it ate into the wall. Deep roaring sounds came from the inflowing water, and then suddenly an even greater roar, as the flow over the top took a large area of wall away with it.

We were watching the gushing waterfall as it cascaded through the breach. It was a terrifying sight: millions of gallons of water was forming its own course through the wall and on along the gully to the next dam.

Within ten or fifteen minutes, the dam was almost empty again. Still standing on the wall, we looked down into a gaping cavity twenty-five feet deep and fifteen feet wide. It would take many days of work with the bulldozer as well as men working by hand to repair the breach. It would leave a weak area, and it takes months for soil to settle and compact.

During a normal rainy season, all the dams fill. It usually takes three or four storms in the right areas to fill them. It was a most satisfying sight to see all the waterholes brimming full. Water birds arrive, and wildlife wander to the edge to drink and don't have to walk far to fill their bellies with the lovely fresh water straight from the sky.

Within a few days of the first rain, green shoots spring to life, and the entire countryside is transformed from its dry dustiness to a lush, vivid green. Later, beautifully coloured wild flowers bloom and pretty butterflies delicately land on their petals. Many kinds of grasses appear and it becomes very apparent when they start to seed. All the birds begin to build their various types of nests. The guinea fowl pair off, and eventually their pretty little chicks can be seen scuttling through the long grass. All the dried-up trees and bushes sprout new leaf buds and, within a week, are glowing with fresh growth.

Yellow-barked acacia trees grow by the dams, their branches being home to dozens of vervet monkeys, who come scurrying down to feed on the new green shoots of grasses and other plants. I was fortunate enough to watch them one evening, greedily stuffing their soft little mouths with mushrooms growing out of a termite hill. They were grabbing hands full and couldn't eat fast enough, the white fungi spilling out of the sides of their lips as they chewed hungrily.

Zebra friskily pranced off as we approached, their bellies protruding full of green grass. The eland were alert, their eyes sparkling with health, as were the sleek impala, leaping into the air, bursting with new energy. Some of the males were mock fighting to see who would claim the herd of fifty or more females. Warthogs ran off, their tails held high in the air like flagpoles, their plump bodies fit and rounded. It is a great joy to see everything happy and healthy once again.

Living where we do, four-wheel-drive vehicles are essential. After heavy rain, the earth roads become virtually impassable, as huge holes and rough, deep ruts appear, and ditches along the road sides become a chasm from the heavy flow of running water. Lorries and two-wheel-drive vehicles become bogged down and often broadside across the road so that nothing else could pass. During these times, we can be held up for hours, and sometimes it is preferable to turn round, if possible, and go back home, abandoning the journey.

The previous owners of our land had built an immense concrete wall across from one rock face of a small hillside to the other to form a rock dam, which is a catchment for water running off a considerable area of granite rocks. The wall was fifty yards across and five to six feet thick at the base, narrowing to a foot at the top of the twenty-feet-high wall. Halfway up it had a strange shaped hole in it, bigger than the size of a man, so it could never fill. Many years after we had been living at Enasoit, we were to learn the real reason for that hole.

Every time there was a moderately heavy rainstorm, the rock dam would fill as far as the gap in the wall, and then flow out like a small waterfall, cascading down over the rock face. There was always a slight seep at the base of this huge concrete bastion, which was welded to the rock with very substantial, heavy steel rods. The hard granite rock had been drilled into and rods inserted, and then the concrete wall was built over the rods, making it incredibly strong. We had asked a neighbour who lived in the area for a very long time what he thought the reason was for the hole in the wall, and he told us that some time back, a young boy had drowned while swimming in the dam. The body could not be removed, so a hole was knocked in the wall to let the bulk of the water out to extract the boy's body. This had not seemed a very feasible reason to us.

At a time when there was very little cattle work taking place, a decision was made to fill in this large gap in the rock dam. Labour was taken to the site, strong concrete mixed, and the hole filled and firmly sealed. The repair was covered with wet sacks so it would dry out very slowly. The wall was, at long last, completed. We waited for the next rainy season with anticipation.

Listening to the rain thundering down, I dreamily wondered what our rock reservoir would look like when the storm finally ceased, and we would drive round to see it. After tea that afternoon, we and a friend ventured round to have a look. What a magnificent sight: a small tarn within the rocky hillside was encompassed by giant boulders and other tiny rock pools and delicately scented wild flowers with raindrops still resting on their pale creamy petals.

We inspected the base at the back of the massive wall; it was seeping out quite badly between the mother rock and the wall itself in several places. I began to feel exceptionally uncomfortable and frightened while standing there below it, so we moved away. I even asked to park the car far to one side of the wall and not directly below it as we normally did. I experienced a very strange aura surrounding the reservoir and its wall, so was very relieved when we left and drove away.

Later that evening we talked about the dam and what a tremendous difference filling in the hole made. It was now holding back three to four times the amount of water. We all went to bed feeling electrified. Sometime in the depth of night, I awoke with a startled shock to hear a very low and deep *boom*, and then the sound of a distant roar, which slowly faded over a period of three or four minutes. I found this strangely ominous, but drifted off to sleep again. In the morning, I discovered that everyone had heard it, and we assumed that one of our neighbour's earth dams in the hills had burst.

The feel of the warm morning sun shining from a clear blue sky was delightfully pleasurable, as were the dew drops on the grass and leaves, which twinkling with reds, blues, and greens like little diamonds. I couldn't resist the temptation to go along with the men to have another look at the brim-full rock reservoir, so we drove around, chatting merrily about one thing and another. My hands flew up to my open mouth and tears started to stream down my burning cheeks as we looked up in total and utter horror at the gigantic cavity of emptiness where the concrete wall had stood. We gaped in shock and hopelessness. The wall was lifted clean out of the rock by the tremendous weight and force of the water, part of it had been deposited forty yards away, and the rest was where we had been standing the evening before.

All the leaves from the surrounding brown olive trees were gone, ripped away by the monumental force of the water, with just the naked trunks and branches showing. Now, and only now, did we understand and realize why there had been a hole made in that wall: the pressure of water when the reservoir was full was far too great for the wall to sustain it. The terrifying thought of what could have happened the previous evening lingered in my mind for many months after.

Driving home late one afternoon, after having been out for the day, one of the herdsmen waved us down. *"Ngombe wote ya Susanna na potea, pamoja na Kini Ebrahim,"* he said: All Susanna's cattle are missing, including Kini Ebrahim, my herdsman. I almost had a heart attack on the spot! All my cattle and the herdsman had disappeared! My entire livelihood. Thinking of the worst possible situation that might have taken place, I was perfectly sure at that moment in time that my Boran herdsman was heading full speed towards the Ethiopian border with all my stock!

As it turned out (and I didn't learn this until the following morning, so I suffered a sleepless night), the cattle had become separated during a heavy storm. Kini Ebrahim had gone home to his hut to avoid getting horribly wet, so the cattle wandered off in several different directions and got lost. When the rain abated, he ventured back out to look for his herd. Of course, most of them were missing, so he was frantically looking for them everywhere. All the other stock on the ranch had come in to the night boma, but not my herd.

When I finally located Kini and my cattle the next morning, I was still furious that he had left the herd to get lost. He, as usual, thought the whole episode was an enormous joke and was splitting his sides with laughter. This melted my anger towards the situation, and I walked away, feeling very relieved at the fact I still owned my stock. He hadn't decided to abscond with them after all.

One of the main problems that can arise when the rainy season starts is bloat in the cattle. After a very dry spell, and suddenly green grass becomes available, the rich damp fodder will cause gas within their stomachs. The cattle can literally blow up like barrels, and the herdsmen have to chase them around to release the gasses in their stomachs. There is a medication known as Stop Bloat that works by pouring a few drops onto a cloth and holding it close to the animal's nose. The gasses within the animal would be released and then the animal would recover. If we weren't extremely careful at these times, the cattle would die very easily.

We made friends with one of the English bank managers of Barclays Bank in Nairobi and his tall, very kind wife. Expecting them for the weekend, the cattle were made available for viewing. Our friends duly arrived, having ploughed their way through miles of mud along the road, their lovely town shoes totally ruined, when they were bogged down and forced to get out and push their car from its stuck position in the wet, gluey earth.

Having enjoyed a delightful lunch, we all went for a drive around Enasoit to look at the herds of stock. Approaching the first group, we were met with the horrifying site of animals lying on their backs, legs sticking up from their enormous, bloated bodies. Driving on to the next herds, we came across much the same situation. Seven animals died from bloat, as the herdsmen had been unable to reach us in time for the medication. After this, we gave each man a bottle of Stop Bloat and some cloth, but it was not easy for them to get close enough to the animals without bringing them all back to the yards, which was not always possible.

It was most embarrassing to have this happen at the very time we took our bank manager around. "Well, Geoff," one of us exclaimed, "we don't expect much of an overdraft after this!"

"Oh," he replied laughing heartily. His eyes sparkled as he trotted off through the bush, his short legs getting tangled in the long wet grass. "You can have as large an overdraft as you like, now that I understand what ranching is all about!" He was happily looking through the rest of the cattle, his round plump face beaming with delight. We were to remain great friends for many years, until they finally left the country.

Gullies were flowing fast with muddy water and overflowing their bush-covered banks, sweeping dead tree trunks and broken branches along. One or two unfortunate animals that had been caught and drowned in the flood, drifted by with bloated bellies. Father and I were searching along one of these roaring seasonal rivers for a lost herdsman, who had failed to return home the evening before. His cattle had all wandered back on their own after it rained without stopping for almost three days. Everywhere was waterlogged and dams were full to overflowing.

The next morning we went out to search again, squelching our way along the boggy ground, the drizzle continuing. The flow of water lessened, but still rolled along at a swift rate. I kept expecting to see a bedraggled, dead body of a man caught up in an overhanging thorn tree or tangled up in bushes where the water swept by, but there was no sign whatsoever of anything resembling a human form—not even a shirt or coat that might have been torn from him in the tumble of water.

Eventually we met up with some of our men who were also searching along other water courses, but nobody discovered any sign of a clue whatsoever. The white mist rolled over the hills and down, like an enormous chiffon cape, and we all were soaked to the skin, cold and shivering.

Back at the labour camp we heard the high-pitched, shrill laughter of women in one of the huts, but also a deeper tone, which could only be a man. There shouldn't have been any men in camp, as they would be out either with the stock or still looking for the lost man. On peering around the door of a smoke-filled hut, there, amid the blue haze and happy women, sat a very relaxed and perfectly unperturbed, smiling man: the very one we all had been looking for and worried sick about for the past two days!

Very relieved that he was alive, but utterly furious that we had suffered so much trauma, he got a well-deserved dressing down. He hadn't even bothered to go up to the house to report his return. The story was that he had become separated from his herd of steers—they being on one side of the gully and he on the other when the flood came down. He abandoned the idea of trying to get home and, instead, walked over to the next-door ranch where he spent two very pleasant and comfortable days with a friend.

Very shortly after we moved into what we called our "Fairy Castle," there was the most totally unexpected and gigantic storm over the house area. Mother was at home, but Father and I were on the hills checking on stock. We saw this unbelievable amount of rain, dark and menacing, arrive from the south, so we swiftly made our way home in the open Suzuki Jeep. Before we arrived we were thoroughly drenched from a howling gale with torrents falling almost horizontally.

Daddy and I were frighteningly worried as we approached the buildings, because we knew that we were still in the process of making the big, wide drains surrounding the house, which we had not yet completed. It was difficult battling our way through the driving storm, but when we reached our front door, the horrific site was devastating. Mummy was standing in a lake of swirling water, soaked to the skin, her hair bedraggled and plastered down. She was weeping hot tears of utter despair and hopelessness. There was a wide brown river running down the steps and through the front door, flooding our grand forty-foot sitting room and flowing out of the side door, which had been opened to let out the hundreds of gallons of water that flowed in under the front door.

Persian rugs were floating and covered in red silt, chair cover bottoms hung in muddy pools, and small ornaments that stood on the rock part of the floor were bobbing about amongst a sea of silt. It was inconceivable that we had just spent the last three weeks preparing the entire place to look so perfect. It had been like an Eastern Palace inside: charming and beautiful. We were exceptionally happy and satisfied with the finish, and now it was in total ruin.

Even the bedroom section was flooded, and we waded through two feet of reddish water in the bathroom. My studio was the only room that wasn't badly affected. We all went to work with buckets, tins to bail the water into buckets, and brushes and cloths. It took us two weeks of very hard work to clear the silt out and wash all the carpets with soap powder and brushes, although they were to remain stained in places for all time. The cement floors were scrubbed but took on a red tint from the silt. We managed to get the chair and sofa covers clean. No one else would ever notice, but we were to see the aftermath of that drastically unfortunate day for the rest of the time we lived in our "Fairy Castle."

Late one afternoon ten years later, I was to return to our splendid home among the rocks, with the silver-haired man who would later become my husband. We had been together on the west side of Enasoit building, our own attractive Mexican-style abode, which would one day be *our* new home. We were met by Mother and Father, who were both looking very pale and somewhat shocked. They related a horrific story.

While at our building site, we saw a dark storm along the Lolldaiga Hills moving towards the house area. Lightning and thunder had been dramatic. One terrific and drastic bolt of lightning struck our home along the pathway to the bedroom section of the house, cracking the walls and knocking crenulations flying off the top of the house. It even cracked the walls in the guest cottages a hundred yards from where it struck the path and damaged the generator for lighting the house at night. One wall in the bathroom was severely cracked from the top to bottom. Father was in the sitting room when the lightning struck and, for a few moments, thought that part of the house was collapsing, the crashing of the strike was so violent.

Horrifyingly, as the storm abated, Mother decided to take an umbrella and move from the sitting room to the bedroom to go and rest for the afternoon. She just entered through the heavy-panelled door of the bedroom hallway when that tremendous bolt of lightning struck the paved pathway that she left only moments before. A few seconds later and Mother would not have lived to tell the tale.

The alarming shock, as the overpoweringly bright light and tremendous noise of the bang hit the path and side of the house, was petrifying. No wonder Mother and Father looked so utterly shocked when we arrived home. I could hardly believe my own eyes when I saw the concrete block crenulations lying all over the path and around the side of the house and the cracks that appeared in the walls. Fortunately, having three-feet-thick granite boulder walls had, without a doubt, protected Mother from the strike. For the next few evenings we were to light our "Fairy Castle with candles until the generator could be repaired.

One morning, just as we were leaving the house to go on a walk, Harun arrived with a most perturbed and urgent look on his usually happy face. "Many cattle are sick," he reported in Swahili.

"How many?" we asked.

"Most of them," he replied.

There were well over six hundred head on Enasoit at the time. The cattle were all standing hunched up, with starry coats, holding their bellies in with pain and scouring very badly. They refused to drink the water in the troughs, and three days later the problem was still a mystery. They simply would not drink water, even though they were making their way to the troughs sniffing water and milling about, but not drinking.

A decision was made to take all the stock along the hills to the earth dam in that area. On arriving, they madly stampeded towards the water and drank thirstily. This was a most puzzling situation. We drained all the tanks and drinking troughs, and then pumped fresh water from the boreholes into them. Before draining them completely, I took several bottles of the water to keep for analysis.

Having pumped fresh water into the tanks, which gravity fed into the troughs, the cattle were brought back to the troughs where they now drank quite happily. This proved that there was definitely something radically wrong with the water. The majority of the stock recovered, much to our relief, and I was insistent that we should get the water tested. We planned a trip to Nairobi and flew down the next day. The Kenyatta Hospital had an experienced chemist who did all the analysis on everything, including water.

The pastoralists who surrounded our area brought in thousands of head of cattle from the north. Their cattle were drinking at the Nanyuki River and at the dams close to where they were stationed. They had come over to us to ask if we could supply borehole water for their stock; it was full of minerals, which, they said, would save them buying salt (which they never bought anyway!), and could we supply the water as "a free gift"! It was just not possible, as the cost of pumping water was considerable. There was simply no way we could agree to this, quite apart from the fact that they would have grazed us out in no time as they came and went. We had no alternative but to say "Sorry" and a firm "No."

The people were not amused with our refusal and, in retaliation, deposited poison into our water tanks in an attempt to kill our stock. Very fortunately for us, there was not enough poison to actually kill the cattle, but it made them very ill indeed. Of course, there was no proof as to who actually committed this contemptuous act.

ENCOUNTERS WITH
WILD ANIMALS

The great elephants and the massive buffalo have given me both excitement and fear on walks through the African bush. They deserve the utmost respect.

—Thelma Hall

Hyena Encounter

The sixty-mile-an-hour gale was still blowing at full force and as hot as the blast from an open oven door, and the tops of a thick canopy of doum palms rustled furiously and noisily. I threw back my sleeping bag; it was eleven at night. Father was sleeping peacefully next to me; we were on a ground sheet. I could see the almost full moon beaming down through the waving palms, dappled light filtering through the violent movement of shadows. We were at Karawi Springs on the northern side of the Chalbi Desert in north Kenya, not far from Ethiopia, this strange and eerie night the 30th of September 1985.

The sweltering heat was too much for me to sleep that night. I gazed up through the palm fronds at the twinkling stars, and then in the distance I heard the whooping calls of hyenas. This made me feel nervous and even more restless, and I pulled my sleeping bag over me again. The liquid cries grew louder and rapidly closer. I broke out into a sweat from the heat of being under my sleeping bag and fear. "Daddy," I whispered.

He woke, and I told him that hyenas were close. He felt that they would just be coming in from the desert to the springs to drink after a hot and thirsty day away from water. I wasn't so sure and grew increasingly fearful. Within seconds, I saw a strange dark shape appear from the shadows, not six paces from my camp bed. I shot up from my lying position, hugging my sleeping bag around me. This huge creature was taller and heavier than an Alsatian dog. Then I saw another emerge into the moonlight on Father's side, and then another and yet another. Before I knew it, we were surrounded by spotted hyenas.

They began making yipping sounds and running around our beds, encircling us. They started to rush in at us from every direction, their tails waving frantically over their backs, eyes ablaze and sparkling red as the moonlight caught them, their manes standing high on the backs of their massively thick necks. Now a variety of most terrifying, blood-curdling cries came from their snarling, frothing mouths as they became frenzied and made their attack. I had never heard anything so chillingly horrifying or ever been closer to a most unpleasant death than at this moment.

We always carried a Browning 12-bore semiautomatic shotgun on these safaris, and there was now no alternative but to use it. The wind was so great that I could not even hear the shots being fired next to me—I just saw the blaze as it burst from the barrel. It was almost impossible to get a clear shot at any particular animal. They were darting back and forth at such speed, and I was in the line of fire when they were on my side. I dared not leave my camp bed, because they would have me in an instant. Some of the big, shaggy-looking creatures would be on Daddy's side and, as he fired, more would dart round to my side again.

They were not afraid of the gunfire. Several were hit and disappeared into the deep, dark shadows of the palms, and the rest continued their attack. We were in grave danger of being torn to shreds and devoured. Running out of ammunition, I made a dash for our little Suzuki Jeep, losing my *kikoi* somewhere along the way and ending up naked. The Suzuki was open, apart from a canvas roof. As I jumped into the seat, a hyena leapt after me but veered off just inches before it reached me, as it was hit in the rear with a blast from the S.S.G.

High winds, hundreds of palm fronds rattling together, and a crescendo of maniacal screams from the throats and still frothing mouths of these utterly frenzied hyenas as they snapped and snarled viciously at us, dashing in and out of the dappled moon-light and shadows, was certainly a living nightmare of horror. I scrabbled about in our bags for more S.S.G. cartridges. Father leaped into the driver's seat beside me, reloaded the gun, and switched the headlights on, whereupon the wild and vicious animals snapped and attacked the lights. I was crouched on my seat in sheer and total terror. We had nowhere to go for protection; they were still trying to get at us through the open doorways.

Father started up the Suzuki Jeep, and we drove towards them to try and chase them back onto the desert. They bounded around the vehicle but were very reluctant to leave it, knowing that we were inside. In these circumstances, my father was incredibly calm and in control of the situation. I was utterly terrified, almost feeling the hyena's great fangs sinking into my naked flesh. For me, it was the most terrifying night of my life.

On my insistence, we collected up all our camping equipment, bundled it into the Suzuki, and moved from the area a mile along the desert to another spring very well known to us. This time, wind or no wind, we erected our tent. I was extremely relieved to be inside and zipped up! By now it was two in the morning. We made a cup of tea, but remained awake for the rest of that horrifying night.

The following morning as the sun rose over the lava escarpment, reflecting its pink glow on the palm fronds, and trickling water flowed out of a nearby spring, it all seemed so perfect, gentle, and peaceful but for the wind. The night's traumatic drama seemed like some strange film or terrifying dream, but it was so real. We had, in fact, almost lost our lives to those hungry hyenas. There is no question whatsoever that, without our shotgun, we would both have been horribly devoured with no trace, other than a lonely little Suzuki Jeep left on the edge of the great Chalbi Desert.

The Bull Elephant

Striding out through the whistling thorn bush along a narrow track, we came to an abrupt halt. Peacefully feeding, his trunk twisted around a succulent branch, was a ponderous bull elephant, his head stretched high as he reached for young, fresh green leaves of an acacia tree. We hadn't been expecting to suddenly come across a lone bull—the rest of the herd was five miles away on the far side of the ranch. The bull was forty yards away when we first spotted him, and he didn't seem to have noticed us.

Within seconds of us stopping, he discontinued feeding and spun around to face us with immense ears spread wide. Backing off quietly, we turned to retrace our steps, but before even reaching five yards, he made an immediate charge at full speed, screaming with rage, his trunk waving back and forth, and his heavy bulk accelerating as he bore down on us. I took off like greased lightning, as fast as my legs would carry me, with Father close behind. We swiftly made our way through the acacia trees, stumbling over the rough terrain, the eminence of the bull elephant rapidly gaining on us, his piercing screams getting louder as he closed the gap. I felt sure that at any moment one of us was going to be trampled into the dusty red earth. I could all but feel his long, creamy-coloured tusks on either side of me. As I breathed hard, trembling with fear and dread, I glanced behind me. The enormous creature seemed to tower over us.

The ground appeared to shudder under the bull's tremendous weight, and I was streaking blindly through the African bush, anything to get away from his terrifying bulk. Finally, Father called to me. "You can slow down now! He has given up the chase."

But I kept on going, determined to put as much distance as I possibly could between myself and the elephant. Half an hour later, exhausted from the run, we reached home. I felt unquestionably weak and looked a shade paler than usual.

It was the first time I had been charged by an elephant while on foot. Father had experienced it on a number of other occasions. We had, of course, been charged many times while in a vehicle, which is to be expected when living amongst wild life.

A Beauty of a Cobra

The afternoon was quiet and slightly overcast with a faint eerie feel to it. I was sitting in a chair in my bedroom, close to my bed, sewing. Not thinking about anything in particular, I became aware of a strange sound, like leaves rustling in a soft breeze, but there wasn't any wind at all. The noise stopped, and I carried on sewing. Then it suddenly started again. It seemed to be coming from under the bed, which was most spooky.

I carefully laid my sewing down, rose and gently lifted the exotic bed cover, peering under the bed. To my complete horror, there, stretched out to its full six-foot length, was the dark shape of a smooth, sleek, and dangerous beauty of a cobra. I jumped back with fright. "Oh my goodness," I exclaimed to anyone who might be listening, "there is a huge snake under my bed!" The problem was how to get it out!

The rest of the family appeared from various parts of the house, and as the snake slithered from under my bed and grace-fully oiled its way along the floor close to the wall, we calmly and quietly stepped behind it and ushered it out of the bedroom door onto the long veranda, where it eventually found its way into a climbing creeper and slipped away.

Shadow or Puff Adder

Many years later, soon after moving into our Mexican-style nirvana home, my husband, Keith, and I had just finished dinner one evening and moved out of our attractive dining room. At the time we only used gas lights and candles. I was barefoot, as I always am when inside the house. Walking towards the steps from our warm sitting room with its glowing fire to the bedroom, I saw a dark shape, like a shadow on the lower step. Instinctively I leapt over it, just missing stepping right on top of a sizeable puff adder, a venomous viper snake!

Born Free Lions

During the early 1960s, George and Joy Adamson were camped with us at Enasoit with a number of their lions, all of which were enclosed within a twelve-foot-high fence, encircling a very large outcrop of granite boulders. Virginia McKenna and

69

Bill Travers were starring in *Born Free*, which was being filmed on Enasoit at the time. *Born Free* was based on Joy's book about her and George's lives with Elsa the lioness.

Very late one cool and bright, starry night, one of our cattle guards arrived at the house with an urgent report that lions were chasing the cattle out of the boma closest to the filming crew's camp. Several herds had taken off in terror, but they couldn't be found in the dark. Father leapt out of his warm comfortable bed, headed for the Land Rover, and motored off to the scene.

On arrival at the stock boma, he learned that the lions were the semi-tame ones and had escaped from the enclosure at the film camp. Father was furious and made his way up the hill to their camp to find out just what was going on. What he found was a roaring party! Nobody was the least bit interested or concerned about the fact that all the lions were out roaming around at will and chasing our stock in all directions all over the countryside! It was two in the morning, and they were all enjoying their party too much to care.

Totally frustrated with the situation and the goings on, Father eventually found Joy Adamson and explained to her what had taken place. She didn't show too much concern to begin with. "Look," Father said to her, "your lions have escaped from their enclosure and are chasing my cattle far and wide over the country. If you are not prepared to do something about it, I shall have no alternative but to go out and shoot them. They are extremely dangerous roaming about like this!"

"Oh," she retorted, "you wouldn't shoot *my* lions!"

The following morning, while most of the film crew were still tucked up in their camp beds, suffering from their previous night's indulgence, George Adamson drove out in his Land Rover, shot a couple of impala, and dragged them behind his vehicle in order to leave a trail of scent. The lions would follow it and eventually end up at his Land Rover, enticed by the smell of meat. This is how he managed to get them all into the back of his Land Rover pickup, drive them back to camp, and encourage them into the enclosure.

Meanwhile, around four hundred and fifty head of cattle were missing. We flew round searching the country for three days, an expensive pastime. A small mob here, another there, and eventually we located them all and rounded them up. Five of the cattle were very badly mauled by these lions; two recovered, but three were so badly damaged with mauled noses, faces badly scratched and chewed backsides, that they had to be shot.

George came over to have tea with us that afternoon, and he was most apologetic. The lions had actually pulled the wire mesh netting apart with their strong paws and squeezed their way out while everybody was enjoying the rowdy party. The film crew was on our property for seven months, during which time we would go and watch them filming on occasion. The film stars lived at the Mount Kenya Safari Club and came out each day for acting the parts. George and Joy were camped on Enasoit near the lions' caged area, which was extensive. The crew also camped close by on the property. They transported the lions in caged vehicles to wherever they happened to be filming.

Fifty-two years later, we had a visit from Virginia McKenna, her son Will, and six camera crew from the BBC in memory of the filming of *Born Free*. They spent the entire day with us at my home, which was wonderful. The crew filmed Virginia and me for a documentary as we were reminiscing. We had the most enjoyable day together. All of us had lunch on my veranda, and everyone felt so much at ease.

Lions in the Garden

The full moon was shining down through a clear, starry night. We were all warm and snug under our duvets. Suddenly, there were scuffling noises outside and the sound of hooves treading and skidding on dry ground. We heard low throaty growls and snarls, and then the inevitable throttling sound of some poor creature being suffocated.

Loud whinnying of a mother zebra for her lost baby was happening just outside the veranda. Andrew, my brother, was staying in the guest cottage on the far side of the lawn and could also hear the snarls and strangled cries from the unfortunate baby zebra. Andrew was able to watch the entire episode from where he was.

There were sounds of heavy breathing, and then the tearing of flesh, munching, and finally the crunching of bones. We were up and standing in the end room of the house closest to the night's drama, trying to see a clear view of what was happening. There were some shrubs hiding our view, but the guttural noises of several lions feeding were evident.

Half an hour later, we watched the three lions rise from their sitting position of feeding and stroll over to our garden fish pond. Crouched down and heads bent over, they began lapping water. We heard grunts and sounds of satisfaction as, one by one, they rolled over onto their backs, legs and large paws sprawled loosely in every direction, and white, full bellies glowing under the still very bright moon. They relaxed until the first soft rays of dawn when they rose sleepily and wandered off into some acacia trees in a nearby gully.

My Bat-Eared Foxes

Wandering back towards the old wooden house each evening after a walk out, I would make clicking sounds as though calling to a dog, but in fact I was calling to wild, pretty little bat-eared foxes—thirteen of them. My foxes, as I called them, would all sit just outside the lawn area waiting for me around six in the evening. When I reached the house, I would give a final call and they would come bounding in as far as the veranda, looking alert and expectant with bright eyes, their bushy tails spread out behind as they sat. Their huge ears twitching back and forth, they waited patiently for little scraps of food that I saved for them.

The situation was unique: I had six wild foxes that I actually fed from my hand. It had taken me the best part of four years to get these beautiful little animals to totally trust me. Some of them were still a little nervous, so they would shy away from my hand, but others were bold enough to take the food from my fingers. It all started after I had put small pieces of bread out on the lawn for the birds. One evening I watched a side-striped jackal gingerly walk up, make a grab at a morsel of bread, and run off with it.

I decided to put small scraps in the same place at the edge of our lawn every evening at the same time. The jackal began coming in fairly often, while bat-eared foxes stood by and watched. Slowly, after a few months, the foxes started to come in and sniff the morsels of food, until finally one evening one fox dashed in, made a grab, and bounced off into the long grass.

Very gradually I moved the titbits closer to the house, and then I would keep out of sight and watch from the veranda. Eventually, both the jackal and foxes associated me with the morsels of food and would sit waiting at the edge of the garden for me to put it out.

I would never want these little creatures to become reliant on me, so I only ever put out very small amounts of food, just enough to entice them in for a short time each evening. Over time, when I threw a piece of bread towards the jackal, he would stand and watch intently. One day as I threw the usual piece, to my utter amazement, he jumped and caught it just as a dog might do! This became a ritual and game for both of us. I would make the arm movements two or three times while he watched, alert and ready, so that when I released the bread, sailing it into the air in an arc, he would dash forward to catch it.

Meanwhile, the foxes watched every movement and so became more and more trusting as they saw the jackal come towards me, with no danger or harm attached. When, after some years, I finally enticed them all up as far as our veranda, I began to sit by the food until I was surrounded by the little furry foxes, the jackal staying just outside the circle to await his piece.

The joy in my heart was total when, after months of sitting holding food in my fingers out to them, one became bold enough and took the titbit from me! To begin with, this did not happen every day. It took a long time, and when the boldest of them got used to this procedure, the others watching became less shy and slowly, but very slowly, more of my foxes started to do the same. I achieved something wonderful and unique, as they were still totally wild and free animals and would only come close to *me*.

A Charging Buffalo

A snort was heard and the sound of something heavy crashing through bush. Here, only ten yards away, an enormous black shape—a very old bull buffalo with nostrils flared and hot, rasping breath almost turning to steam as it met the cool morning air, his head with its huge heavy boss and widespread horns worn at the tips from age—lowered his head and came straight for us at full charge.

There was no time to step out of his way; there was no escape route for us whatsoever. He came at speed down the narrow gap between boulders and dense bush. In a split second, he was upon us, slamming his rough, massive boss and all his solid weight into my father, who was just two steps in front of me. Had I not been there, Father may have been able to leap aside and avoid the charge, but with me being right behind, his first thoughts were, if he did, then I would be in line for the buffalo's charge, so he stayed in front of me.

Instinctively, Father put both hands up and onto the huge animal's boss. The buffalo used all his power and bulldozed my unfortunate father, pushing him over backwards and through thick, heavy bush, and then proceeded to gore him three times, relentlessly smashing into Daddy's ribs, arms, and thighs. I was kicked amongst the rocks by his powerful back legs, which were pounding the ground as he pushed forwards at great force, dust covering me as one of his rear hooves slashed me across the right knee, and I tumbled over.

Picking myself up, I looked around me in a daze. Suddenly, the huge black bull was no longer there. I staggered towards the horrifying sight of Father lying sprawled out on top of rocks amongst bush. He was completely covered with blood, and both arms were just raw, red flesh from where the buffalo had ground away with his great knobbly boss, leaving a torn, mangled mess. Looking down, I felt shock and horror thinking that Daddy must be dead. He couldn't possibly have survived such dreadful blows.

"Oh, my God ..." The words were music to my ears coming from Father's blood-stained lips. He was alive! It was the 28th of July 1996 and we had been on our usual morning's walk. I could feel the blood pounding through my veins with shock at what had just taken place over the past thirty seconds. I gently pulled Father up and onto his feet. One trouser leg had been completely ripped off by the animal's wide horns, leaving a very bruised and lacerated leg and thigh showing. He had a badly cut face, wounds of shredded flesh, bruises, and a number of broken ribs where the bull had forced Father's binoculars into his chest.

"I will run home and fetch the Range Rover for you," I said.

"Oh, no, no. I will manage to walk. It is only a mile or so," he replied.

We both staggered slowly home, presenting my mother with a ghastly shock and, consequently, had a later breakfast than usual! We ran a warm bath so Father could soak all his wounds, and then we bandaged up both arms, which were severely damaged from elbows to wrists, and gave him medication for pain and bruising and antibiotics.

There was no way that Father would entertain the idea of going all the way to Nanyuki over rough roads to see the doctor. "Susan," he said, "you and your mother can do whatever needs doing. We don't need a doctor." It took several months for all the wounds to heal and ribs to repair themselves. Yet another narrow escape ...

It turned out that this poor old bull buffalo was also chasing our cattle men around. He was becoming very dangerous, and we felt that the time had come to do something about him. It would only be a matter of time before he killed someone. Three days later, sadly, but inevitably, he had to be shot.

Two Buffalo Bulls

Strolling along one morning in open grassland, and near a rocky outcrop two hundred yards away, there was just a single thorn tree on the ridge that Father and I were walking along. Suddenly we heard the sound of pounding hooves, and over the north end of the ridge came two, large, black bull buffalos at full gallop. Being in open country, there really wasn't anywhere to go, so we stood still where we were, hoping that they would divert past us. This was not to be: they came towards us, puffing and snorting as they bounded along. We made for the tree, and they galloped round the tree after us! We were now all rotating round and around the short, stubby acacia. Where ever we went, they followed.

Eventually, turning to face them head on, we both threw up our arms and made gruff, growly noises and clapped our hands, whereupon the huge, dark, hefty beasts turned tails towards us and charged off in the opposite direction and over the southern side of the ridge.

A Wounded Buffalo

Three hundred and fifty yards from our old wooden home we created a salt lick and small game pool, which was filled from a pipeline extending from the house borehole, in order to encourage the wildlife. Some ranchers believe that buffalo bring disease into their livestock, and so discourage them by shooting them. We were fortunate enough never to experience this problem, but were unfortunate to have a wounded bull buffalo with a great spread of heavy horns drinking at the pond early one clear, warm morning. We hadn't realized at first that he *was* damaged.

Returning from a walk after having checked on the cattle, we were two hundred yards from the house when the bull spotted us from where he was drinking. Without any hesitation, he made an immediate charge towards us. We took off at a fast run, and he quickly gained on us, but as he came, we noticed that his left rear leg was faltering. He was extremely angry and it became obvious that he was suffering severe pain. The wounded buffalo almost reached the garden before we did –we had only just made it onto the veranda in time. Watching him turn in a circle, sniffing the air with contempt, head held high, it appeared that he was dragging his left back leg at intervals, probably shot high up in the rump area. Later we learned that a neighbour had, in fact, shot and wounded a bull buffalo. On contacting him, a game scout was sent over, and the poor unfortunate animal was finally shot dead.

A Rhino Charge

A family of three was visiting me: friends from the southwestern part of the United States of America. I had shown them an abundance of African wildlife while they'd been staying, but we hadn't yet come across the black rhino. So I decided to take them over to see a friend and manager of a neighbouring game sanctuary. Asking Mike if we could motor around the area on a game drive to look for rhino, he very kindly offered to take us out in the company's Toyota station wagon, which had substantial roof hatches for the sole purpose of game viewing.

After a very welcome cup of hot tea and Marie biscuits, we set off motoring slowly along through beautifully scented, flowering *acacia mellifera* trees, one of many different species, as opposed to our *acacia drepanolobium* on Enasoit. From behind an enormous granite boulder, which would have rolled down from higher up the hills many hundreds or even thousands of years ago, appeared a small family of shy, sleek greater kudu: two cows, one with a pretty young calf, its large brown eyes with long lashes watching us intently as we moved by, and huge, patterned ears twitching to keep flies away; and a beautiful, stately bull, his spiralled horns tipped ivory colour.

Around the next corner was a small herd of buffalo, which cantered off as we approached, the little dark-brown woolly-looking calves bounding happily after their mothers. Driving down from the hill area to the lower country, there were fresh rhino droppings scattered about and spoor along the track. Mike ventured off into the bush and drove across country and over rough terrain to look for rhino. We were all standing with our heads out of the roof hatches catching the cool evening breeze. Somewhere amongst thick bush, and very close by, I heard quick, heavy breathing and puffing sounds above the noise of the engine.

"That sounds like a rhino!" I exclaimed. "I think we are in for a charge any moment."

A few seconds later, out of the bush charged a full-grown female rhinoceros, her head down and long horn pointed straight for us. Her breathing became faster as she puffed her way towards us like an express train.

Mike put his foot down on the accelerator to move off, and, lo and behold, we went crashing down into an enormous ant bear hole, the front right-side wheel truly stuck! At that moment, the cumbersome body of this huge female hit the right-hand side of the Toyota, rocking it so violently that we thought she might turn us over.

Snorting loudly, her breathing getting faster and faster, she backed up a few feet and rammed us again and again! The vehicle rocked back and forth as we all got thrown from one side to the other. I thought her extensive horn would come straight through the side door as I peered down over the roof hatch, inches from the top of her enormous head!

Eventually, bouncing our way out of the sizable hole, the engine revving loudly, we roared off across country out of her way. The last view we had of our annoyed rhinoceros was the bulk of her plump backside and waving tail as she pounded her way off in disgust back into the dark bush from where she had come. My guests were extremely surprised and enthralled. They never expected the excitement they had just received and would, no doubt, dine out on the story forever more!

Baboon in the House

My bedroom door, which led out onto the veranda, was open, and the warm afternoon sun was streaming through. I was sitting browsing through a field-guide bird-book when I suddenly noticed a shadow pass by. Very strange, I thought, as I knew Mother was resting on her bed and Father was in the office. The shadow reappeared and, to my horror, an enormous dog baboon walked through the doorway!

I leaped to my feet to chase it out, but it turned and walked out on its own, rather like a tame dog would have done. I called through to Mother, who immediately came, and we both went out to the veranda. The great woolly beast was in the patio area, and, seeing Mother and me, it bared its huge fangs, its brows back and eyes round and aggressive, it came for us at a gallop. We both ran back towards the bedroom door, but, unfortunately, Mother slipped and went crashing down onto the floor. When I ran back to assist her, the shaggy creature jumped upon the veranda wall, which was two feet and six inches high with a variety of pretty coloured, semi-precious stones laid along its top. A number of these fell to the floor, making a crashing noise, which, fortunately, deterred the baboon from coming any further. It backed off and went careering around the house.

I hurried to the office to get Father. He came straight over to the house and got out the pump-action shotgun. Unbeknown to us, the animal had, by this time, got itself into the house through the kitchen door, which must have been slightly open, and was hiding, we discovered, behind one of the white wing-chairs in the sitting room.

The hairy monster dashed out from behind the chair. As it did so, Father fired, but the baboon moved too fast, so the chair was shot up. Father pulled the trigger a second time, but the gun jammed, and the furry creature made a leap for Father and tried to get at his face, whereupon Father held up the gun horizontally to protect himself from the attack. There was a tremendous struggle between man and beast, the baboon biting into the stock of the gun with its huge yellow teeth. During the desperate outburst of commotion, they ended up crashing through the door and into the bedroom, Father still trying to keep the vicious creature, with its fiery eyes and bared fangs, from his face and neck.

Finally, with great difficulty, Father managed to shake the animal off and hit it over the head with the butt of the gun. It was stunned to some extent and scurried underneath my parents' bed where Father, having managed to release the jammed pump action, shot it. Remember that we were living in the old wooden house at the time, which had soft board walls lined with papyrus matting. My bedroom was on the other side of the wall where the baboon was shot. Opening my wardrobe drawer to find a skirt two days later, I discovered that all my clothes within that drawer had been shot up. S.S.G. pellets had gone through the baboon, through the wall, into the back of my clothes cupboard, and into the clothes drawer!

Another Baboon

Another baboon incident occurred when two big males were insistent on hanging around the house and wouldn't stay away. They seemed to be just too tame, like the previous one that got into the house. Whether they were used to human habitation and had come in from somewhere else we will never know, but they can be a very dangerous animal when they lose their fear of man. The big males have eye teeth almost the length of lions.

After a few weeks of these two baboons coming in close to the house, one disappeared leaving the other, which continued to stay close. Trying to chase it away didn't work, so the decision was made to shoot it once and for all. Father was outside trying to find a position suitable in which to shoot it, which was not easy when the animal was staying close to the house walls.

I was trying to locate the baboon from the inside by peering out of different windows. Suddenly, spotting the baboon close up to one of the sitting room walls below a window, Daddy, from outside, let fly with the shotgun, totally unaware that I was inside that particular room peering out! The S.S.G. pellets hit the baboon all right, and came on through the wall near where I was standing and went whizzing past me within a couple of inches and out through the far wall.

Even as I write, large troops of baboons are a constant nuisance to us, as they come close to our homesteads to feed from garden plants and flowering trees. During the afternoons after the house staff leave and everywhere is quiet, I close the outside doors while I am in my studio writing or painting, just in case we get another unwelcome visitor.

Only two years ago, while enjoying three days in the Nakuru National Park, four of us were contentedly having a picnic lunch up on "Baboon Cliffs," which is a designated picnic site. A troop of baboons came close by, and one big, furry male watched us eating and made a beeline for me. He leaped onto my left shoulder with terrific force (at a guess, they must weigh in the region of seventy to eighty pounds), and then onto the picnic table and stole away with our bread rolls. I was left quite badly bruised and a little shaken. I am most unamused at the fact that people will insist on feeding these wild baboons, which can cause terribly dangerous situations.

The Young Lion

The young lion still had spots around his paler belly area and a small fluffy mane, but he was fully grown. He had, over a period of five or six months, killed a total of forty-six head of cattle, including seven of our own. Everyone who owned land in and around the area was after him. He had become a stock killer.

One night, during the month of April in 1966, we heard the sounds of stampeding cattle; they were in a paddock close to the house. Then we heard the typical noises of an animal being suffocated and the throaty growls of a lion. Father leaped out of bed and drove off in the vehicle to the scene, where he found the dead steer five hundred yards from home and the young lion beginning to feed. We had given this lion many chances; it had killed two steers a few nights before and some previously. He looked so beautiful with his big yellow eyes looking up from his meal and staring into the car lights. His face was covered with blood as he began to chew into a thigh, licking a juicy part with his rough, pink tongue.

Daddy aimed to shoot, and then slowly lowered his rifle. *I will give him one more chance*, he thought and fired into the air to scare the lion off, just hoping he would go and not return, but this was too much to hope for.

At four in the morning the lion returned. Instead of continuing to feed from the steer he'd killed earlier in the night, he killed yet another one. This time the aim was to shoot to kill.

"Let me get this over with. I hate to do it, but …" Father aimed along the barrel of his rifle and saw the big, woolly head buried into the meat. As the lion lifted his head to gaze ahead, his eyes narrowed, and, for a split second, man and beast looked intently into each other's eyes. The trigger was gently squeezed tighter and tighter. *Boom!*

At seven-thirty the following morning, two vehicles arrived with professional hunters and ranchers aboard. "Have you seen or heard of a stock-killing lion?" they asked. "We are after him and have searched all over for him."

"Have a look behind my store," Father replied dryly.

They all piled out and walked over to the store. "Well, I guess the hunt for this fellow is over," one of them said. "Well done, John."

"Oh, I didn't intend killing him, but in the end it seemed there was no alternative. Such a shame really."

The hunters and ranchers clambered back into their hunting cars and drove away. To this day, we still have the skin of this unfortunate lion, but never was another lion shot on Enasoit.

Lioness with Cubs

She was living on Enasoit with her cubs not far from the house. From what we observed, she was the sole hunter for herself and her family. It must have been difficult for this lioness, and we felt for her. Walking along the track, which led to where the rock dam used to be, we suddenly heard a very loud and distressing warning growl coming from behind a nearby bush. The lioness was there with her cubs and must have felt that we would walk right into her. She saw us, but we didn't see her.

We stopped and very slowly stepped backwards for a few paces, and then turned and retraced our steps back towards the house. If one of the cattle happened to die, we would put it out for her. It did help her tremendously, because she would feed from the carcasses and take her cubs along too. We would see their spoor and the evidence of their having chewed at the meat. Eventually, they all moved further away from the house area to enjoy their lives in the peace of our land.

Side-Striped Ground Squirrel

While still living in the wooden house, we mostly ate breakfast and lunch outdoors in our patio area. The superb starlings became so tame that they would prance about on the table and peck the bacon rinds from our plates while we were still sitting there. One thing leads to another and, seeing the birds happily surrounding us, a little bushy-tailed, side-striped ground squirrel started to come close to the table at meal times. Offering him titbits, he also became very tame and eventually would take food from our hands.

One lunch time while enjoying eating a wonderful jam roly poly Mother had made, the little squirrel scuttled right up to gaze at her. He stood on his hind legs and sniffed the air, his tiny nose twitching from side to side. Mother spoke to him, as she always did, and handed him a piece of her jam roly poly, which he took gently in both his weeny hands and, sitting with his fluffy tail bushed out over his back and head, proceeded to eat his piece with great relish, his round, bright eyes sparkling with pleasure. When he'd finished, he looked at his sticky little hands, and then licked the last of the jam roly poly from them before scurrying across the dry, brown lawn.

Clara, the Yellow-Necked Spurfowl

Another visitor to our outside dining table was a female yellow-necked spurfowl. My mother named her Clara. Like the squirrel, she had watched the birds come in without fear and finally mother was able to feed her by hand. She would peck away at whatever she was offered from the palm of Mummy's hand. Clara would always go round to Mummy's side of the table, obviously knowing her from anyone else. Straining her skinny, wrinkled neck, she would come out with her raucous, high-pitched squawk, which went right through one's head, asking for titbits.

"Chuk, chuk, chuk," Mother would call, and Clara would come running across the lawn at full speed for whatever morsels were available. Then, all of a sudden, Clara was no longer around, and we all assumed she had been taken by something. Mother would call and call, but no Clara.

Quite some while later, we were just finishing lunch inside the house when there was a strange scuffling sound. Turning towards the open, double front-doors that led onto the veranda, what should we see entering but Clara, followed by five chicks! She came strutting up to Mother's place at the table, craning her neck. She expressed herself with her usual squawks, while her chicks scuttled their way round the sitting room, sliding about on the polished floor.

A Fiery Eyed Leopard

Leopards on ranches often take young calves if they have the chance. At one time we kept a small herd of milk cows and their calves just to provide milk for ourselves and the labour. One such leopard became very bold and started to go for the calves at night, one after another, until we felt that something had to be done about it.

A knock on the back door late at night and the cattle guard reported, yet again, that this particular leopard just jumped into the calf boma and made off with another one. Driving down to the stock enclosure with his rifle, Father decided that he had better look for the calf killer. He parked the Range Rover a short distance from a yellow-barked acacia tree, the headlights still on and shining onto the rough bark, a glow filtering up to the canopy and network of smaller branches and leaves. There were fresh claw marks on the trunk, and a blood trail existed where the leopard had taken the calf up to drape its prey over a suitable branch.

Father walked closer to the tree, the stockmen behind a few yards. He looked up into the mat of branches and there, looking down at him with eyes of fire, crouched the large spotted cat, its sleek body and glossy coat darker than many of its kind. It glared into Father's eyes, its own ablaze with fury at having been disturbed. Suddenly, without any warning, the leopard sprang with determination and purpose out of the tree directly at Father. His immediate and automatic reaction took but a split second: lift the rifle, aim, and fire. The beautiful creature crumpled in mid-air. Tumbling down, it fell with a loud thud as it hit the ground inches from Father's feet.

He bent down slowly and stroked the soft damp fur of the dead leopard's cheek, eyes beginning to glaze over, one life extinguished but the other saved.

Wild African Hunting Dog Encounter

On one of Africa's hot, sunny afternoons, we scrambled over a low, rocky outcrop, its interesting bushes in full bloom, and reached the summit to look over at the vast Laikipia Plains. A cobalt-blue sky was dotted with cumulous clouds, like white puffs of cotton wool, and a soft breeze caressed our flushed cheeks. Stepping up and over the last of the boulders, there facing us was a small pack of wild African hunting dogs, their large rounded ears twitching and their noses high, sniffing our scent on the warm air, their tails waving from side to side.

We came to an abrupt halt as the black-and-tan-patched dogs began to move towards us. I had fully expected that they would turn and trot off in the opposite direction, but they started growling, a low menacing sound, and then curled back their lips in an ugly snarl as they continued to come forward. Initially we stood our ground, still believing they would back off, but this was not the case. We were the ones who finally had to retreat, and they still followed, keeping up their throaty growls.

Throwing some sizeable pebbles at a boulder to make a "bang" was the only action that stopped them from pursuing us. They stood across the rocks in front of us with sparkling eyes set in their wide faces, their black noses continuing to sniff the air and their heads moving from side to side and bobbling up and down, wondering whether to pursue us further. We turned slowly, keeping a keen eye on them, and headed back down the koppie and away to the grassy plains below.

Four Hundred Elephants in the Garden

A circle of enormous wrinkly bottoms was the view we had from our lawn looking across one hundred and fifty yards to the circular water tank. There were well over two hundred elephants taking turns to drink. Their trunks were over the tank wall sucking up water, and then their heads tilted upwards, their curved trunks trickling the water down their throats. It wasn't too long before the tank was empty. Then they all made their way ponderously over to the lawn and our fish pond.

A short while later from the other direction came two more herds of elephants. Their entire population decided to meet up on our lawn. Now there were nearly four hundred elephants all milling around and making the most incredible sounds as they met up and greeted one another, the babies playing, and the mothers feeling other youngsters with their trunks. Huge bulls with long, heavy tusks stained yellow with age, met up with others they knew, but hadn't seen for some time. It was the most fantastic sight we ever witnessed. And from outside our front door!

To try to protect our walled-in garden and the fish pond, Father stepped from the veranda and walked thirty yards to the pond, thinking the elephants would move away, but they took not the slightest notice. They surrounded him and continued to suck up the water and fish, which they promptly blew out of their trunks onto the lawn to wriggle, struggle, and gasp their last breaths. Mother and I were totally amazed watching the elephants walk past and around Father, as though he were just another elephant.

Unable to do anything about saving the garden, the pool, and surrounding plants, Father walked back through the elephants to the veranda, where we just stood and gazed in awe and wonder over this most amazingly wonderful scene. It was almost getting too dark to take photos, but I did manage to get a few shots.

I decided to walk out onto the lawn. The magic of this spellbinding scene captivated me to a degree. To have such wonderful creatures surrounding our home was unbelievable. There was one extremely large bull elephant who turned to look at me. He stood very still and was at peace with the situation. I very, very slowly crept towards him. At twenty feet from him I stopped. We just looked at one another. I was totally enthralled. He was so majestic, and his tusks were mighty. After standing so close to this fantastic animal for quite some time, I finally ambled back to the veranda. The huge bull looked from us across to his fellow elephants, but remained for a long while in the same spot, himself transfixed by ourselves and all his kind.

The herds enjoyed our garden for the rest of the evening and, indeed, most of the night, uprooting all the plants, chewing up the sisal, and spitting out the fibre after having consumed the juices. The noise of rumbling tummies, deep throaty expulsions, and screams as mothers controlled their young was all quite terrifying while we lay awake in our beds, totally surrounded by hundreds of gentle giants.

Elephants, for their size and weight, are extremely gentle creatures, but one is bound to notice a change in the area where they have been feeding, particularly when over four hundred have been in one's garden! The total destruction of our garden the following morning had to be seen to be believed. It looked as though the Third World War had taken place on the lawn. But the elephants never touched the house at all.

We were left with the most tremendous mess to clear away after these massive phantoms of the African continent had taken themselves off to the acacia trees down in the gully a short distance from the house. It took the ranch pickup, my Suzuki 4 x 4, the Range Rover, and many men four full days to clear away the debris, dragging masses of chewed up sisal plants, branches, and leaves from the pepper trees, torn up bushes, bougainvillea, and trampled plants. Yet another experience of a lifetime.

What was once a most attractive garden and walled-in fish pond area remained bare, bleak, and devastated for the rest of our time at the old wooden house, which was probably a year and a half before moving up to the "Fairy Castle."

The Three Baddies

Apart from the large herds of elephants, there were three very big, fully grown, but young bulls with enormous tusks who lived together and frequented our garden at night. Strangely, elephants love eating pepper trees, which are actually an imported tree from Australia, but grow very well in Kenyan gardens. The three bulls would always come together. Mother named them "The Three Baddies."

There were lots of potted plants on our veranda, and these three extremely naughty giants would gently put their huge trunks over the veranda wall and feel for the most succulent ferns. Finding something tasty, they would pluck the unfortunate plant out of its pot. Sometimes the greenery would be firmly situated in its soil, so the whole pot would be lifted up, and then crash. It would smash into pieces, sending soil everywhere onto the veranda floor. The shock of the noise would wake us. Until this kind of incident took place, the elephants would be extremely quiet and careful not to damage any part of the house. They would always know when they had done something really naughty and sneak off around the side of the building, remaining silent.

To try to protect our pot plants and the garden, we would get up and shoo them away, except that when they heard the heavy wooden bar being lifted off the double front doors, they would hurry off across the lawn and hide behind various trees and shrubs. They would remain silent so we would think they had gone. As soon as they heard the wooden bar, which was our door lock being replaced, they would immediately return to the veranda to resume their tactics.

On one occasion, Father was beginning to get a little annoyed at having to keep getting out of his warm, comfortable bed to chase the "baddies" away from the plants, so he went roaring out shouting at them to "Push off!" and shooed them across the lawn, whereupon one bull turned, ears spread wide, and chased him. Father scampered back towards the house at top speed, losing his colourful striped kikoi along the way, the cool breeze whistling around his now naked body as he reached the safety of the veranda.

The three never came close during the daytime, but would come in at around ten or eleven in the evening just as we had dropped off to sleep. There was an old, sizable pepper tree growing very close to my bedroom window, which I mostly had open. One very clear and moonlit night, strange noises at my window woke me up. There seemed to be a huge shadow blocking the sky and stars from view. Throwing back the sheet, I crept over to the window to peer out right into the chest of an elephant bull. He was standing less than eight inches from my window, reaching up with his trunk above the overhang of the corrugated iron roof and collecting choice leaves from the pepper tree. The branches were being pulled up and down, making a scratching sound on the roof. I felt totally intoxicated; I could have put my hand out of the window and touched him! It was just incredible that I should be standing in my bedroom as close as this to a live wild elephant!

Fighting Buffalo

I could hear the thudding and crashing of boss against boss from my bed. The moon was on the wane, and the stars were bright in a clear night sky. Suddenly there was the sound of splintering wood as one enormous bull slammed his great head and horns into the other, who was pushed backwards into our guest cottage, his wide rump blundering into one wall.

We were in the process of building a second guest cottage and had just dug a very large hole in the ground, fifteen feet deep and six feet across, for the toilet sump. After what seemed

Susan M. Hall

ages, the buffalo fight came to an abrupt end, and I dozed off once more.

In the morning we discovered one wall of the guest cottage had been quite badly damaged, but the most terrible thing had taken place. One of the bulls, a magnificent young creature, had obviously been pushed backwards and had fallen into the toilet hole. He was alive and gazing up at us with wild and terrified moist eye as we peered down at him.

There was no way of getting the bull, with his dangerously large horns, out alive. It would have put people at great risk of being killed so, most unfortunately, he had to be shot. Then there was the problem of getting him out afterward.

The tractor driver was sent for and asked to bring the big Fordson County Super Six, which he parked close to the hole. Then men clambered into the hole to secure a substantial rope around the unfortunate buffalo, which was then hauled out slowly. It needed real power to lift the heavy body up and out. If only we could have got him out alive. But how?

Elephant Incident at Samsara

After purchasing one of these extraordinarily amazing mobile telephones, which was an alien piece of equipment to me at the time, I received a voice message from my neighbour in the Shimba Hills, inland from the South Coast. There had been a problem at my Samsara house.

My property borders the Shimba Hills Game Reserve. An elephant from the reserve, happily feeding from one of my cashew nut trees, as they often do, had stepped backwards onto the concrete top of my loo hole. His weight being far too great for concrete, it had given way and he had gone down the hole. Very fortunately, there had been other elephants in my garden at the time, and somehow they had managed to help him out, leaving a large collapsed loo hole.

"What do you want to do about it?" my neighbour Dick had asked. He very kindly offered to put some of his chaps on to repair it for me and I said, "Oh, yes please!"

90

When I next went down to Samsara it was all nicely repaired, and thereafter we put large lumps of spiky coral around the concrete top to prevent elephants from stepping on it again.

Mongoose in My Boots

My leather boots with their soft inside lining were always parked in the evenings by the bedroom door on the veranda of the old wooden house. One night, before retiring to bed, I heard a scuffling noise, so I peered out of the window. There, climbing into the boots and out again, was a pair of white-tailed mongoose. Their white bushy tails were waving to and fro over the tops of my boots. This took place most evenings, so I had to make sure that I always left the boots in the same place for them to play in. They had the most wonderful time, and I couldn't help but smile to myself watching them.

Friends in the Bush

We were surrounded by elephants, all with their trunks waving in the air scenting the aroma of fresh damp earth that Father and I were digging from the side of the ranch track to fill ruts and holes recently created by heavy rains. I became a little apprehensive as they closed in on us; they were all very curious and came to within a few yards of where we were working, no aggression was shown, just curiosity. It was amazing to be side by side with these gentle giants out here in the wilderness of the African bush. They showed no fear of us, and slowly I lost any fear that I initially had of them. These elephants stayed round us for the duration of our work and only moved off when we finally got into the open Suzuki Jeep and drove slowly away.

Leopard by My Window

I awoke to strange mewing sounds outside my bedroom window. The moon was bright, and I slipped out of bed and tiptoed towards the window. The curtains were always pulled back, and I could see the silhouette of the Lolldaiga Hills. Just below the window, only a foot away, were two magnificent leopards, their spotted coats glowing like soft velvet as they moved beneath the silver moonlight.

They were playing and caressing one another. The two were obviously male and female very much in love. I was totally mesmerized by them and stood watching for twenty minutes and more before finally returning to my now cold bed. I lay there smiling to myself with pleasure at having experienced such a wonderful sight, and then drifted off to sleep.

Sambo, the Colobus Monkey

When I was a little girl of five, we acquired a baby colobus monkey. He was already black and white when he came into our lives, though they are born pure white. I am not sure how old he was but he was a small baby anyway. I loved him dearly. Sambo would curl up on my knee while I gently brushed his long, soft fur and go to sleep.

As he grew older, it became increasingly difficult to let him roam around the house. He would take the flowers out of the vases and eat them and dip his tiny hands into the sugar bowl and lick the sweet sugar off his fingers. Sambo loved bread and milk, which we fed him in his own special bowl.

Finally, a large wire netting cage was erected around a tall-ish tree and he was happy to live in there for a while until he learned how to undo the wire door. He had watched Father open and close it, and he knew just what to do.

There were a number of very tall gum trees growing near the house in Happy Valley, and Sambo decided to spend time high up in the these trees, and then come down at night and sleep close to the chimney where it was warm. Sambo loved Cape gooseberries and would come walking with us to the kitchen garden to gather them. He would get most annoyed if he thought you had eaten one more than he had and would look at you with wide eyes and make an "O" shape with his mouth. This meant that you were not allowed a single one more than he.

Sometime later he took to calling to the wild colobus who lived in the forest close to the house. He also started to feed himself on the leaves of natural forest trees. By the time we were to leave Happy Valley to move to Nderit Estate in the Great Rift Valley, Sambo had almost become a wild colobus. There was no way we could now take him away from the area; he was living as a wild monkey, even though he visited us often. It was sad to leave. He had become part of our lives.

Calling to the Mourning Doves

There is a bird call, which, amongst several others, always reminds me of our safaris in the Northern Frontier, and that is the call of the mourning dove. I can imitate this dove, and on numerous occasions when camped by sandy riverbeds in the North, I used to walk along and call to the doves. To my immense surprise and delight, they would follow me, first one way along the river bed, and, when I turned to retrace my steps, they would follow me back, and all the time we would be calling to each other. It gave me enormous pleasure. I felt so much a part of the wonderful nature around me.

Mother and father (Thelma and John)

Susan at home

Susan M. Hall

The crashed Bonanza aircraft, VP-KHU

96

Cattle outside the spraying yards

Cattle grazing

My own cattle and herdsman Kini Abrahim

Cattle coming into the yards

Mother and father (Thelma and John) on safari, sitting under the shade of Doum palms, Chalbi.

Our home at Enasoit Ranch

Susan M. Hall

Mother and father (Thelma and John) with Gabra people in the Chalbi desert

PART TWO
SAFARIS IN THE NORTH

OUR FIRST SAFARIS

Come o' cool night, Come hither breeze from the desert, I know the scent of you now. Rouse the camels in the night before the little wind of dawn.

— Kahlil Gibran

It was Christmas 1979. The last minute loading completed, we left the ranch, just the three of us: Mother, Father, and myself. We were heavily loaded with camping equipment, food, water, and petrol to last us for ten to twelve days with some extra rations in case of emergencies—one could never be sure just what might take place in this wild and rugged land.

Moving steadily along the stony road, I looked back towards the ranch. How dry it was, I thought. The grass had turned almost grey with the drought conditions. I hoped that everything would be all right until our return and that our stock wouldn't be stolen by the neighbouring tribes.

Three quarters of an hour later, we approached the small town of Nanyuki. I was shocked yet again at the neglect of the place: the rather dirty looking street and general shabbiness. It didn't take long to fill up with petrol, and then we were off. The safari had begun; just one of many that we experienced and would continue to do so in the future.

We were now travelling on a tar road for the best part of sixty miles. Climbing to eight thousand and five hundred feet above sea level along the slopes of Mount Kenya, through the wheat growing area, we could feel the cool fresh breeze coming down from the great snowy peaks. The air was crisp and clear, the snow glistening in the morning sun. It became warmer as we descended, passing the last of the lush green fields and entering thorn bush country.

We travelled from over eight thousand feet down to three thousand feet at Isiolo, a small outpost on the border of northern Kenya, in just half an hour. One was very aware of the altitude difference. There had been rain a few days previously, and the grass was beginning to turn green, although the atmosphere was now dry and hot. Leaving the tarmac road at Isiolo, we headed north into Kenya's vast Northern Frontier. The road, now very corrugated, became thicker with dust as we approached the drier country, the fine white powder filtering into the vehicle onto our hair and skin. Isiolo, the last place for getting any fuel, was well behind us. The dry desert country we headed into was uninhabited by any Europeans, just the tribes who were seen wandering on foot in their traditional dress.

In the distant blue haze, Ol-Olokwe, a huge, square-shaped mountain, beckoned us and, as we drew closer, its magnificence increased. Our first night was spent beneath its imposing bulk. Looking directly up four thousand feet from where I was standing, I could see tiny black specks circling round the great granite cliff face. They were vultures, and this wonderful place was their home where they roost at night and had a superb nesting ground. The enormity of the cliff face was so awe inspiring, and the colours of the granite were a deep tan splashed with orange and streaked with black and white—the white being bird of prey droppings.

The relaxation after the day's dusty journey was a delight. We would take a long walk into the valley between the mountain and the lower hills that surround it. Tall acacia trees presented lovely cool shade, and the many varieties of beautifully coloured birds twittered and called in the branches as we passed beneath. Various types of magnificent wild flowers, still in bloom, desperately held onto their last small quantity of moisture from the rain a week before. Within a few more days, the hot sun would dry everything out and the petals would fade, and then fall to the ground and wither.

The sun sinking behind the bulk of Ol-Olokwe left us in total shade, and the stroll back to camp was undisturbed. A cool drink of shandy quenched our parched throats. The evening drew to a close while I watched the smoke rise from our newly made campfire and drift lazily past the tent. When the coals turned red, a piece of wire mesh was laid over them, and we roasted fresh meat for the evening meal.

We heard the distant grunt of a leopard, and later a lion roar, probably marking his territory, and, finally, much closer and clearer, the call from a hyena echoed in the valley. Crickets and night flying insects joined the evening sounds. The stars were bright and clear; the African night was advancing.

The vivid red sky of dawn reflected onto the enormous crag, turning it to a gentle pink as the vultures flew out from their crevices to catch the thermals and drift even higher into the sky in search of food, perhaps the remains of some animal killed by a lion or leopard.

Chill was taken from the air as the sun rose over the distant hills in the East. A raven settled in a nearby tree, hoping to find a few morsels left over after we had eaten.

Continuing north, the road as dusty as it could be, we passed the odd herd of goats here and there with a young child to guard them. To the east sat an eternal plain of scrub bush, and to the west, the Mathews Mountain Range stretched for sixty miles, its northern extremity sloping down to the wide Milgis River bed. The river is mostly dry but flows after great rains in the mountains and separates the Mathews from the Ndoto Range. Little puffs of white clouds appeared in the pale sky as the heat rose from the parched land and met the cooler air above.

Laisamis is another small outpost consisting of a few buildings and a Catholic mission. Leaving the road north, we turned west along a sandy track, hardly more than a camel trail. Crossing the Milgis River bed much farther to the northeast than where it passes through the mountains, it was dry. If it had been flowing, we would have been unable to cross due to its depth and thick muddy brown silt, which it carries along.

Looking towards the west one could see the Ndoto Mountains, pale and distant, towering above the heat haze like giants rising from a deep sleep. Some way beyond the Milgis *lugga*, we passed Baio, a massive mountain, its eminence surrounded by the Kaisut Desert. As I cast my eyes towards its summit six thousand feet up, I could just make out the huge rock jutting out like a needle, a great overhang right at the top. I longed to climb this beautifully shaped mountain every time we passed it. I would look longingly up at the awe-inspiring cliffs and, indeed, make a plan in my mind to do just that one day.

The going was always very slow along these rough tracks. They were hardly ever used, but it did not matter to us, and it was a delight to be able to enjoy the magnificent environment surrounding us.

Soon the Ndotos took on a more prominent shape. We were not more than just over two thousand feet above sea level, and the summit was almost nine thousand. The closer we got to the mountain range, the clearer everything became. I could see the enormous granite cliffs topped by juniper forest. It all looked so very green up there, compared with the hot, parched scrub land we were travelling through. Needing a drink, we would pour water from a canvas bag tied to the front of the vehicle. The water was comparatively cool, having caught a little of the breeze as we moved along.

By midday we were well into the mountains, and it was time to stop under a shady acacia tree and have lunch. While sipping cool homemade wine taken from our portable fridge, I gazed in wonder at the huge mountains rising over six thousand feet above us. I enjoyed reaching Illout, a place where the Rendille nomads come with their camels to collect water from the wells. There are many dry, sandy riverbeds heading out from the mountains. It was one of these that we decided to drive up and spend the next few days. We must have travelled for five miles along the sandy surface passing various types of thorn trees on the banks when finally we came across a really old acacia, a wonderful shade tree, and set up camp.

It had been a long hot day, but we felt ready for a good walk. What a beautiful place this was surrounded by the foothills of the great Ndotos. Rocky outcrops here and there were just asking to be explored, or so I thought, as we made our way along the riverbed. I longed to climb them all, but the area was so vast that it would take months to explore, and we were only going to be here for a few days this trip. Heading back towards camp we saw the spoor of a male lion. The big prints spread out in the soft golden sand were about a day old. Later, Father and I collected some wood from the dead and fallen trees to make a campfire. Gathering together a few small sticks and handfuls of dried grass to start it, the strike of a match, and the flame soon burst into life.

The elongated shadows gradually faded as the sun tipped the blue line of the mountains and disappeared, leaving the clouds tinged with pink and mauve. The crescent moon was already glowing, its neighbour, a single twinkling star, changed from green to red and gold like a sparkling diamond. The lonely hoot of an owl portrayed peace and tranquillity. As the fire died down, I wondered what the rest of the world would be doing this Christmas Eve. I awoke to the musical sound of many birds, even the ravens were calling. Stepping sleepily out of my tent, I sat in a camp chair to watch the sun rise over the lower hills, its glow already reaching the tops of the mountains to the west.

After a leisurely breakfast, we walked along the riverbed looking to see what animals had passed by during the night, leaving their tracks behind in the sand. A variety of trees were in flower, including the beautiful desert rose, its deep-pink-to-almost-red flowers and pale centres standing out against the dry, brown scrub; its thick, stocky trunk giving the appearance of a miniature baobab tree. I gathered some of the blooms, the sticky milk-like substance running down the bark as I plucked each stem. These, together with grasses and some pretty coloured seeds arranged in a jar surrounded by small pieces of quartz rock, made a very attractive Christmas decoration.

Back at camp we lazed in the shade of the acacia, the sun, by this time, being very intense. Even the Grant's gazelle and little dik-dik were standing in shade some distance from our tents.

A sudden thud out of the tree startled us. There, lying on the ground, was a dead lizard, twisted and shrivelled about thirty inches from head to tail and looking like a miniature dinosaur. It must have died some while ago, and the wind had dislodged it, causing it to fall from the tree.

Our lunch was a little different from the traditional Christmas meal, consisting of cold chicken, green peas from a tin, slices of creamy avocado pear, chopped raw cabbage, dates, raisins, slivers of cheddar cheese, and pickled onions. Closing my eyes I had visions of this being served on beautiful Wedgewood dinner plates and drinking the cool Black Tower wine from thin-stemmed cut glass. Coming back to reality, I soon discovered that we were using yellow plastic plates and tin mugs. The brandy butter—taken straight from the car fridge and rapidly turning into a thin sauce as it met that midday heat—was delicious poured over the plum pudding.

Later in the early evening, a long walk was called for. Wandering across country, the scrub bush scratched our legs as we passed. Climbing a small hill strewn with granite boulders, we had a breath-taking view: the distant mountains were still shimmering in the heat rising from the Kaisut Desert. To the northwest, Mount Nyiru and the Ol-Donyo Mara mountain range were in view, and way beyond, directly north, between eighty and a hundred miles away, the pale outline of Mount Kulal, which rises from the shores of Lake Turkana, previously called Lake Rudolf. We were surrounded by the most magnificent mountain ranges.

The evening sun was just touching the horizon as we arrived back in camp after walking along the sandy *lugga*. The sky, clear and pastel blue, merged into soft pink that deepened to blood red as the fiery ball disappeared, putting an end to another day.

The gentleness of dawn crept over us as we packed up camp to continue the journey north. Moving slowly down the *lugga*, we watched dik-dik scurry off, their little noses twitching as they peeped from behind trees. A giraffe, reaching up and delicately nibbling the Acacia leaves, moved off as we approached. Crossing over the Illout and South Horr track, we continued along the riverbed until we met a camel trail heading north across the Korante Plains and the Hedad country. This trail, sometimes used by missionary vehicles, is passable by 4 x 4 vehicles most of the year round but would be very difficult during the rains. Granite outcrop formations were fascinating; sparse clumps of grass bleached almost white by the desert sun wavered to and fro in the northeast wind. Rosy-patched shrikes flitted from bush to bush and a lone jackal trotted by.

In some areas we had travelled through, there were still traces to be seen in the sand from our previous safari four months before; no other vehicle had passed during that time. Heading in a westerly direction now, we made our way deep into the foothills of Mount Nyiru at the north end of Horr Valley. Dark clouds grazed over the mountain top, and then swept down towards us. The huge, deep-blue mountains on either side of the valley were rapidly being shrouded with rain as the sky turned to dark grey and the heavy clouds rolled in. The air became cooler but only a few drops of rain reached us.

Much later, as the evening progressed, twinkling stars began to peep from behind dark clouds. A cool wind caressed our backs, while in front we absorbed warmth from a campfire. The low chirring call from a nightjar and the echo of baboons barking on some nearby rocks drifted into camp on the night air.

After preening his feathers, a mourning dove took off, flew high into the morning air and out of sight. Sunbirds of varying types could be heard chittering in the branches and, as they flitted about, the sun, catching their tiny bodies, made them shine like precious jewels. A swoosh of wings could be heard as a Verreaux eagle flew by searching for hyrax along the outcrops of rock, his black plumage looking like velvet against his contrasting white rump. His mate, circling several hundreds of feet above, kept a watchful eye on his movements.

Leaving behind the beauty of Horr Valley, we entered lava country, which contained mile after mile of dark boulders and a cone or crater here and there. The immensely hot sun beat down, and the wind blew dust in swirls across the lava plain and in through the open windows of our vehicle, settling in our eyes and hair. The closer we got to the lake, the greater the gale force winds. Stopping for a drink of water was quite an ordeal: the mugs almost blowing out of our hands before we had chance to fill them with deliciously enticing water from the canvas bag. One had to hold the mugs way to one side in order to catch the liquid that was being blown as soon as it left the bag.

Just before the escarpment, the magnificent Lake Turkana came into view. The great Jade Sea spanned approximately one hundred and eighty miles, its eastern shores strewn with dark, hot lava boulders that the sun heated to an untouchable temperature. They reached to the water's edge and beyond. We descended very slowly, bouncing from boulder to boulder, sometimes crashing into enormous holes. Once we reached the shore, the going was a little easier, although it was all shale. The hot winds were even greater now and there was not a tree in sight, only the eternal black rocks giving off tremendous heat.

It was a relief to end our travelling for the day about six miles from Loiyangalani. With great difficulty, due to fantastically high wind, we managed to erect a canvas sheet to create some shade. The lake looked so enticing, and we couldn't resist a bath in the cool, jade-coloured water. What a pleasure it was to wash one's hair and clothes after days of moving through that dry, dusty country.

Sitting in-between rocks, we felt reasonably safe, although we still kept a keen watch for crocodiles that cruised up and down along the lake shore. Most of that afternoon was spent in and out of the water to keep cool. Our skins turned a rich golden brown, my hair bleaching blonde in the intense sun. The constant gale was still hot and burning our faces as the sun sank out of sight behind the hills on the western shores of this great lake. The light became softer, the pinks and blues of the sky reflecting on to the water. Removing the canvas shade due to even windier conditions, we set up our camp beds behind some large boulders and covered them with smaller rocks to prevent them from blowing away until such time as we retired for the night. As soon as darkness fell, scorpions of varying sizes crept out from under the rocks, some several inches long and pink in colour. These creatures carry a very nasty sting.

We lay on our beds looking up at thousands of bright, twinkling stars, the hot wind blowing constantly, and lava dust filtering into our eyes, hair, and sleeping bags. It was really too hot to sleep. I would have lain on top of my bag, but for the fear of scorpions crawling over me during the night. It certainly wasn't the most comfortable night I had ever spent, and it seemed ages before I finally fell asleep.

Dawn found the wind still blowing with great force, as it always does along the eastern shores of Lake Turkana. We had a hasty breakfast of cereal before moving off towards Loiyangalani, where fresh spring water seeps from out of the ground. There is a small trading centre there, a number of Turkana and El-Molo huts made from palm fronds, a mission station, and a small lodge where visitors flying in by light aircraft to fish from the lake may spend a night or two. By eight in the morning, the heat is fairly intense, and already the tribesmen around Loiyangalani were lounging in the shade of the palms that surround the spring.

Continuing north again through many miles of lava strewn desert, the conditions became even hotter. Towards midmorning, we entered an area where the black boulders burning with heat lessened and gave way to sandy gravel with sparse bush. Eventually the bush came to an end and we reached the Chalbi Desert, where the dust is so fine that it blows up in clouds as one travels along. The Chalbi Desert is a flat salt-pan area, like an old lake bed, and the mirage caused through immense heat, made it look like a great lake merging into the sky with no horizon. Everything shimmered and was very distorted and out of focus, leaving one feeling a little unsteady.

It was midday when we reached the first of a series of springs, Kalacha Dida, which flows gently from out of the lava plateau, which meets the Chalbi Desert. Under the shade of the doum palms and out of the wind, we relaxed for a while after the hot journey from Loiyangalani, with a mug of cool wine to refresh us. Dates, a slice of cheese, and an oatmeal biscuit always serve as an adequate lunch in desert conditions. Some miles farther east, a spring came into view, one we had camped at on our previous safari. And again, our tyre marks were still visible in the sand.

The small spring, belonging to a Gabbra family, was most attractive surrounded by palms and green grass. The cool water with all the shade around presented a most peaceful setting. Here, we planned to spend two days. After getting the camp organised, it was simply blissful to wander through the seclusion of the palms and bathe in the wonderful fresh, clear spring water.

The isolation of the area suited me perfectly. The only humans for many miles were the elegant, high-cheek-boned and long, slit-eyed Gabbra family, who come to the spring once a day or every two days to water their camels and goats and collect water in goatskin containers for themselves. They lived a mile or two from the spring on the lava plateau in small huts built from the doum palm fronds, which are wonderfully cool inside. In severe drought conditions, they sometimes moved closer to the springs so their stock could spend more time grazing the green grass beneath the palms. The grazed grass can grow as much as two or three inches during the night due to the very hot conditions and the seepage from the spring, so, by the following day, there is again enough for the animals to graze on.

The livestock usually live off the short scrub that grows among the lava boulders, but when this dies out, they are forced to feed round the springs. On this particular safari, we hardly saw the family at all and were left totally alone. It was almost as though we owned the little area ourselves.

The evening was delightful, still very hot but not unpleasant. Frogs began croaking in shallow pools as though telling each other of the day's events. The clear sky had a soft-pink hue all around and, one by one, stars began to twinkle. The gentleness of desert evenings are something more than beautiful. The moon reflecting onto the palm fronds as they caressed each other in the breeze whispered sweet secrets that I longed to share. Peace reigned over the entire desert. This was truly one of the happiest evenings of my life.

***

On a number of these exciting and pleasurable safaris into the north of Kenya, my brother Andrew joined us. He found the wild country fascinating, too. While Andrew was working for a gemstone company, he was detailed to go up to look for geodes north of Loiyangalani.

Following Andrew on one of his geological safaris—he in a rather battered, old Land Rover pickup with his men who were working for him, and we in the Range Rover—we bounced our way across the roughest country full of rocks and deep sand in places, with no roads or even a vehicle track in sight. It was incredibly and unbearably hot, and the going was uncomfortably tough.

We all camped north of Loiyangalani near Porr Hill. The semiprecious stones and geodes that Andrew was to collect were in an area four hours' drive north of Porr Hill. We used maps and a compass to find our way across the wild and uninhabited country. Andrew had one of the local tribesmen with him to help show us where to go.

The idea was to leave the camp at five in the morning, and then struggle our way along sandy riverbeds and open, rocky country. The cloudless pale sky allowed the full force of the African sun to beat down upon us with its overpowering heat. Everything that one saw was shimmering and distorted in shape. As soon as we reached the area, work started. The right type of rocks were collected, one by one, and loaded carefully into the vehicles. The rocks were heavy and burnt our fingers as we lifted each one, the sun having already penetrated their hard surface.

What looked on the outside to be the most mundane-looking, yellowish and greyish rocks, when broken open turned out

113

to reveal the most fascinatingly brilliant amethyst and quartz crystals, which had been lying there intact and unseen for millions of years. Now they were glistening in the scorching morning sun like fiery diamonds, and we were totally mesmerized by these stunningly beautiful sparkling gems, which changed from one colour of the rainbow to another. As we turned them in the light, their facets caught the sun for the first time since they had been created.

The rocks were loaded, whole of course, to be cut professionally once they arrived in the jewellers shop in Nairobi about five hundred miles from where we were collecting. One or two were cracked open on-site to check what kinds of crystals would be going for sale.

All around us it was flat, treeless country dotted with sparse scrub bush. It was so incredibly hot that we were forced to move out by noon and head back to camp. The rocks would be unloaded to wait for the trucks coming from Nairobi to pick them up.

Five days later, we were exhausted from the dry intense heat and the travelling to and fro over such rough terrain to collect and load the rocks. Our hands were sore from the work. When there was enough for a truckload, the rocks were put into fifty-gallon drums and the tops sealed to await transportation.

***

The weather was warm but cloudy with storms around. Lightning flashed across the entire Chalbi Desert, and thunder created a very eerie feeling way out north of the Chalbi and towards the Hurri Hills along the border with Ethiopia. The winding track was narrow and hardly ever used. Bouncing from one large puddle to another, the earth, a rich red, was as sticky as glue.

The puddle ahead was longer than some but didn't look any worse than many we had come through, the cloudy, grey sky reflected in it. As we entered, the heavily loaded Range Rover sank rapidly and abruptly, lower and lower, until we were tilted on our side and came to a halt. The wet, gluey mud oozed up the side of the right door, and there was now only one way of getting out of the car. One by one, the three of us clambered out of the large Range Rover window, our bare feet and legs sinking into warm, deep mud. It only rains but once a year in the Chalbi Desert area, and we had just arrived at the wrong time in March. After this experience, our future safaris were planned to avoid the rainy season. The horror on our faces was never recorded, but I do have a slide transparency of the Range Rover, which was to remain firmly stuck for the following two days.

Being midday by this time, after clearing a space and having moved many of the hot, black lava boulders aside, our first move was to unload the camp table and chairs and situate them by the side of the track.

After our lunch, which included a large tin of mixed fruit, Mother and I, using the empty fruit tin, began to try to bail out the water from under the car from one side while Father dug a trench to drain it on the other. What seemed like hours later, I discovered that the water we were laboriously bailing out had been flowing happily back down the newly made channel and out, but then trickled around the corner of the car and back to where it started. So our afternoon's work proved fruitless.

The three of us were exhausted by dusk and now had to clear an even larger area of ground from all these beastly boulders in order to put up our three-man tent for the night. Collapsing into our sleeping bags and still covered in drying mud, we slept intermittently. The calls of hungry hyenas could be heard close by in this very remote and lonely land.

The following morning the sun was shining brightly. There was just a very sorry looking Bahama Gold Range Rover sadly stuck in deep, watery mud up to its windows. Shovels full of gluey mud were thrown aside and more water was bailed out. By mid-afternoon on the second day, Father dared to try and drive the car out of the enormous hole it was wallowing in, now dried out to some extent from all our efforts.

Slowly, with the V-8 engine revving a little higher than normal, its power pulled it out. Mother and I were rejoicing. The

Rover eased out about ten feet, only to plunge yet again into another gluey mud hole! Our sense of humour now totally failed as we started the process all over again.

After finally getting ourselves out the second time, we were fortunate enough to find within the lava boulders two beautiful, deep, clear pools of fresh rainwater. It was sheer bliss to strip off our thoroughly mud-caked clothes and sink into the cool, delightful pools. Washing our unpleasantly dirty hair was a real luxury. The water from the previous day's rain was trapped in the rocky depressions, so it proved to be a perfect bath. Normally, water in this desert area is very scarce, the only water being from the springs in certain areas, which bubbles out of the ground. Springs are few and far between, particularly in the lava country.

Between this strange and lonely area north of North Horr through to South Horr, roughly one hundred and twenty miles over almost impassable tracks winding through desolate and rough country, it became quite an epic trip due to seasonal rain and ended up taking us a week. In many areas along the way, we were forced to rebuild the track where it had been badly eroded away by the floodwaters and make detours around places that became ravines. There was water flowing, golden-brown, froth from the rapid flow attached itself to bushes in every gulley and sand *lugga* after the heavy rain on Mount Kulal, which was a good thirty miles away from where we were at the time of crossing these waterways.

Dark, rolling storm clouds grazing along the upper slopes of the bleak Mount Kulal looked horribly ominous. More rain was to come. There was no other way to get through and out of this wilderness, other than to try to cross the flowing rivers. If we didn't, the chances would be that we could be there for many days, and food would run short.

The Range Rover, the only vehicle in a hundred miles or more, was laboriously unloaded. Everything was taken off the metal roof-rack, fuel and water cans were untied and removed, and all heavy items from the inside were taken out to make the overweight automobile lighter. Mother and I watched in great trepidation as Father, in the Rover, entered the first of these swirling eddies three hundred yards wide, the track heading off around a sharp bend. The muddy water reached up to door level as they disappeared round the corner. We could hear the *bloop-bloop* sound of the exhaust as it sank below the murky surface of the river, and then silence.

The relief was tremendous. Father returned on foot through the torrent of brown liquid, his trousers soaked to above his thighs, but the car was safe on the far side. Now there was the task of carrying everything through and to the other side of the river barefooted. The stones, gravel, and thorns beneath the water, cut into our feet, which were unaccustomed to this kind of treatment, and we stumbled in and out of holes, the current pushing us off balance. It proved impossible to walk through in shoes, which just slid off in the slippery mud.

Equipment held high, some of it carried on my head, we struggled through what seemed an impossible situation, carting everything to the far side of the seasonal river to reload the vehicle. Many trips were made back and forth by the three of us, until we had carried everything. On the last tramp through, the river started to rise again. We had just made it!

***

Towards the close of another incredible safari—this time, being extremely dry and hot, too—as we travelled east through the Kaisut Desert, Baio Mountain close on our right, heading for a small outpost called Laisamis, which was still another two hours' drive over rough country, the track was hardly visible in places.

Way ahead in the hazy distance, we saw clouds of white dust billowing into the morning air and being blown by a high northeast wind, and dark specks moved along in front of the dust and were coming rapidly towards us. It was a very strange sight in the middle of this extremely desolate, uninhibited area. The only people we ever saw were the nomads as they passed through from time to time with their camels in search of new feeding areas for the stock. As the specks grew larger, the vision of vehicles appeared in the waving heat—a most ominous perception.

It eventually became apparent that it was a convoy of open-Jeep-type vehicles, with four to five dark skinned men in each and wearing jungle-camouflage clothing, with green, rounded steel helmets and heavy black lace-up boots. They carried special ladders for crossing sandy or difficult terrain. The first of these strange vehicles drew up close. The following one parked right in front of us, preventing us from moving any further, the next one parked behind, and yet another parked on our left. We were totally surrounded, trapped; there was no getting away, the rest still heading towards us. There were nine vehicles, and each and every man carried a firearm.

The paler-skinned man in control spoke English. He was taller than the rest and had broad shoulders, fine aquiline features, defined full lips, and very cold sparkling dark eyes. Mother and I glanced at one another in horror as this cruelly good-looking man gazed through the car windows, examining everything within before finally setting those cool black eyes first on Mother in front of the car, and then on me sitting in the back. Mother and I were both wearing short dresses made from kikoi material, the heat being the deciding factor of our attire, and there was nothing readily available to throw over our bare, suntanned legs. I became very nervous wondering just what was going to happen next.

The man stepped out of his vehicle with his rifle and swaggered his way up to Father's open window. He rested his large, brown hands on the side of our car, and he had another, more intense and curious look around the inside, and then he proceeded to accuse us of being in the area for the sole reason of poaching elephants. He finally dragged his gaze from us to settle it on the roof rack for some moments, and then his furious eyes darted back inside the car, which was fully loaded with all our safari gear. The arrogant young man suggested that we were hiding the ivory inside the Range Rover!

Father gave him full permission to search if he wanted. Not that it was any of their business, but they were heavily armed and made that point quite clear. The perspiration was now gently trickling down my face, more from nervousness than the hot sun, which was beating down upon us. Eventually, after what seemed an eternity, giving a last hard stare, he said in English, "You are free to go." He then jumped into his Jeep, started it up, and drove away. The rest of the convoy followed, leaving us slightly bewildered to say the least! Heaving a sigh of relief, we continued on our way.

Later in the day, when we reported the incident to the Kenya authorities at Laisamis, then Isiolo and later still, Nanyuki, they didn't have the slightest idea who these strange and unusual-looking people could possibly have been. They most certainly were not from Kenya.

***

The view of Lake Turkana, earlier called Lake Rudolf, from its southern escarpment is overpoweringly stunning. Travelling through the barren lava-strewn and treeless scenery, devoid of any form of life that one can see, is almost like a moonscape. All of a sudden, over yet another bleak lava ridge, there in front and below in the middle distance, lies the Great Jade Sea, another of the Rift Valley's amazing wonders, shimmering like a bright illumination under the heat of the African sun.

The vehicle track at the time was incredibly rough and the escarpment frighteningly steep. There was an area known as The Steps: lava ridges with a drop of two-to-three feet in places. The poor automobile would literally drop from one level to another, jolting us about, up and down, and side to side, like a jelly on a plate. We'd ease along a few yards, and then drop off the next step, seven in all down to the bottom over a distance of several miles.

The country below and along the empty lake shore is covered in a thick, grey lava-shale. Nothing penetrates its harsh surface in the way of vegetation; it's bleak, bare, and parched. The odd bush or small tree that manages to survive is bent over to an extreme towards the southwest, like a gnarled, lonely old

119

man struggling for existence in the tremendously high winds almost all the year round from the northeast.

Unbeknown to us at this time, the howling gales of the area lessen their strength for a few hours each day around noon, giving a very false sense of security. We thought the calm situation was normal, not realising the gales were constant, except for a few days in March during the rainy season. This was one of the first of many safaris to come. Over the years we were to learn all about this wonderful, desolate, and, in some areas, inhospitable country.

Arriving at the exposed shore, we stopped for a much-desired drink of water from the canvas bags tied onto and hanging from the side door of the car. Heat from above, and from the lava stones below, was immense and has to be felt to be believed. Each blast of hot wind was like the furnace from an oven, burning our skin in minutes. The light of midday was dazzling and turned everything into a shimmering white blur that made our eyes water, even through the slits of a squint. Conditions were too extreme to feel like travelling further. Clearing an area of the lava gravel, we erected our tents next to the one and only, sparsely leafed, lonely acacia tree. It afforded little shade from the overhead scorching orb of the sun. We ate a light lunch, too lethargic to feel hungry, and then tried to rest on our camp beds inside the tents. Dozing on and off in our own perspiration, which soaked our pillows, dehydrated us.

The cool water of Lake Turkana, although jade in colour, was thoroughly irresistible. We all wandered down to the water's edge and, in great anticipation, unable to resist any longer, plunged in it! What a tremendous joy and relief from the excessive heat. It was unsafe to remain in the water and relax, as large crocodiles were gliding gently along just below the surface and close to the shore. The evening drew on while we reclined in camp chairs, gazing in wonder at the magnificent colours—delicate pinks and purples—of the sky after sunset, the huge billowing cumulous clouds, a pale saffron, reflecting into the still waters of this vast lake.

A gentle, warm breeze drew attention from our dream world. Suddenly, a strong gust blew one tent down, and Father and Andrew re-erected it; Mother and I shared the second tent. We all retired to bed after the intense heat of the day. As we lie awake, the wind became stronger, and both tents collapsed on top of us all. Struggling around in the jumbled mass of canvas in the dark, I finally found the zipper, opened it up, and Mother and I crawled out into a hot blast of gale-force wind. Father and Andrew had done much the same. The sky was as clear as a bell, and the stars shone brilliantly down on us. Between them, the menfolk managed to put both tents back up again, struggling to secure them by tying the guy ropes to the Range Rover, the howling gale now even greater.

There was no chance whatsoever of getting any sleep. We were all busy hanging onto the tents and ourselves from being hurled along and into the lake. Our tent made the most awful tearing sound as it ripped its way out of our hands and tore from top to bottom along the edge of the zipper. The strong canvas behaved like fine tissue paper against the most terrifying gale.

Dawn approached with the violent turbulence of the wind still at full force. We managed to roll up the partially collapsed tents, the camp beds and sleeping bags, not to mention the pillows, which, by this time, had taken off towards the lake with Andrew after them at speed. Then we bundled them all in a screwed-up heap into the vehicle with great difficulty, the tremendously powerful wind making it almost impossible to hold open the large Range Rover doors, which slammed into our backs with a harsh thud as we wrestled with the camping gear, our hair taking off and standing on end. My hair was tied into a ponytail, but had long since escaped the hair slides and was blowing in every direction, mainly in my face and eyes. Settled eventually in our seats, we made our way north to the tiny African village of Loiyangalani, situated close to the lake and by a spring, the doum palms breaking some of the high wind, and then carried on towards the Chalbi Desert and the rest of our safari.

A real mirage is something unbelievably spectacular. The most amazing sights I have been fortunate enough to have witnessed were in the flat salt pans of the hot and windy Chalbi Desert. A few years ago, the elegant, nomadic Gabbra people would cross the

Chalbi with their camel trains from the southern side to the north, where springs of clear, sweet water bubble from the ground beneath a mass of beautiful green and swaying Doum palms, to water their stock and collect and carry water back to where they live. Some of the tribes live close by, others thirty miles or more away.

The Gabbra carried the water in their goatskin bags, which were made by the women and strapped to the sides of each camel. The women, who strode across the desert beside their camels, were wearing a piece of printed cloth (*kanga*) of varying colours, but sadly faded from the scorching sun. The Kanga was tied over one shoulder and clung to the women's slim bodies in a very strong gale of around sixty miles per hour. The men, wearing soiled white turbans and long, baggy shorts made from *Americani* (calico), with a piece of the same material slung across their shoulders, brought up the rear.

Watching these camel trains move across the Chalbi from a distance of a mile or so, the people and camels appeared to be gracefully floating, dancing, and quivering through the air in the stark midday heat. It was fascinating, a mirage of long thin streaks wobbling uncontrollably. They could have been anything—the shapes unintelligible, dark apparitions shimmering as they drifted along above the horizon as though in a vast lake.

As we drew closer, the shapes took on a more prominent form, until eventually they met with the waving horizon and were no longer elongated or suspended. Even one tiny bush could give the appearance of a large spinney of trees.

Sadly in many ways things have changed over the years: boreholes have been established in a number of areas putting a stop to the nomadic way of life. They no longer need to trek the great distances for water, which, in turn, means that their areas become more grazed out and trampled by stock, and the people become lethargic and bored.

***

It was on another of these wild and fascinating safaris that we were, again, camped on the east side of Lake Turkana. The distances are so great and the going extremely slow, so we would inevitably end up for at least one night by the lakeshore. We had a fairly large tent, called a *ngong*, a style of tent named after the Ngong Hills, that can sleep the three of us: Mother, Father, and me. Due to high winds, yet again, we fastened the nylon guy ropes securely to the Range Rover to prevent the tent from being blown over. The tent pegs would not stay locked into the ground, it being deep and soft lava shale. The wind would drag on them, and they would pop out. The tent was parked about fifty yards from the rippling water's edge. Lake Turkana's water is not too pleasant to drink, being fairly brackish, but is perfect for bathing in and washing clothes.

We needed to refill our Jerry cans, and this was a perfect opportunity. Father leaped into the driver's seat of the Rover, started it up, and moved off towards the shore. We all quite forgot that our tent was still attached! A nasty ripping sound occurred as the tent left its position and was dragged along the hot shale surface.

Before we could erect it again, poor Mother had the miserable job of trying to repair it. Sitting in the overpowering sun (there is no shade at all along the lake) and stitching the tough canvas with a thick needle and heavy thread, the thumb and middle finger of her right hand became increasingly sore from pushing the needle through such thick canvas. She wept with frustration; it was not our idea of fun at all. Meanwhile, I was helping to fill the water cans and load them back onto the roof rack.

***

One calm, pleasant evening, camped below the enormous bulk of the flat-topped mountain Ol-Lolokwe, we were sitting peacefully in canvas camp chairs and sipping wine, with a most welcoming fire burning gently, its coals glowing in the fading light, when suddenly there was a piercing scream from an elephant, and then the rumbling sounds from others all quite close by. As it grew darker, we could just make out their gigantic black forms, like phantoms, as they moved about, in and out of the surrounding bush.

Mother, nervous of elephants at close quarters (from past frightening experiences), took to sitting in the Range Rover. The fear put her off her supper. I was nervous myself, wondering just how close they would come to our little camp. By now we were surrounded. They didn't bother us at all, however, and we retired to bed, quite relaxed. Eventually, they wandered away, deeper into the African bush.

Much later, lying down and listening to other, pleasant night sounds, we heard distant roaring from a lion interspersed with intervals of silence. The roaring sessions kept coming closer until it was in our camp area. My heart beat faster, and we could hear him sniffing the air. Peering out of the tent window, we saw him standing a few yards from us, the bright, glowing moonlight shining onto his golden fur and whitish lower legs and feet. I snuggled deeper into my sleeping bag hoping he would stay a reasonable distance from our tent, but the next minute he was sniffing loudly at the canvas near my ear less than an inch from my head—there was just that thin cloth between his head and mine! I was motionless and dared not breathe. Moments later, Mother looked out of the thin mesh window only to come face to face with him looking back in!

***

Walking along the dry, wide *lugga,* with the clean, pale-cream sand landing in our shoes as we moved along, we watched soft bluish shadows lengthen as the desert sun slipped down gently behind the deep-purple mountains, creating a pink hue across the western sky. I climbed up the *lugga* bank to cast my eyes across the most magnificent scenery.

Suddenly, a deep roar, and then movement of what looked like a golden body behind the bush I was standing next to. I leaped back into the riverbed, my face somewhat paler, according to Mother. It is extremely easy to walk up on sleeping lions when in the African bush.

There are plenty of other kinds of life on the move in desert country, not the least of which are scorpions, thousands of them. Each time we roll our tents up after camping for a night or more in the same spot, these lethal creatures scuttle out from underneath and run in all directions. Large pink ones looking like miniature lobsters, their tails curled over their backs, are ready to attack and sting anything unfortunate enough to be in their way. Smaller black ones, more poisonous than the pink variety, also scurry about. They all pack a very nasty and exceptionally painful sting. George Adamson's brother, Terrance, once told me that he'd never experienced greater pain than a scorpion sting. As I write, our family has managed to avoid being stung. If one's shoes are left out of the tent, scorpions will happily crawl inside. I would much rather find a lion sitting outside my tent than scorpions, which look so incredibly evil, not that they are, but it's not so funny if they get into one's tent or sleeping bag.

Suzuki Safaris with Father

After having been on a number of safaris in our Range Rover in northern Kenya with Mother and Father, and sometimes my brother Andrew, I was extremely inspired to explore more of the wonders of the hot, wild and immensely interesting deserts and the vast and beckoning mountain ranges. My admiration of the uninhabited lands knew no bounds, so I was very determined to go back and explore these amazing places, which meant driving for many miles or even hundreds of miles through country without roads or even tracks, but across rough terrain through unexplored areas of wilderness. It also meant walking and climbing some of the many mountains to achieve some of my ambitions.

This was not my mother's ambition at all, but Father was very excited at my suggestion of exploring further. Andrew had thought it a good idea that Mummy might enjoy staying with him in the Old Town of Mombasa, where he was living at the time. She would be able to go out and paint the wonderful scenes, which she loved to do. And, indeed, she did enjoy the change.

The old buildings and the narrow streets of the Old Town inspired Mummy. The Arab and Swahili ladies dressed in black *buibui* (the covering veil of Muslim women) and long gowns, with only their large, dark, alluring eyes showing, and the rest of their faces and bodies covered. The scent of oriental perfumes graced one's nostrils as they glided past. There were also delicious smells of spiced cooking coming through open doorways. Some of the men were in turbans while others wore little Muslim skull caps, and all wore long, white *kanzus* (the long-sleeved calico robes). Some slowly ambled along the streets, talking to one another, while others sat on concrete seats outside shops or their homes, sipping spiced Arab coffee and eating sweet *halua* (sweetmeat).

Mother painted many of these delightful scenes on canvas while she was staying with Andrew, while Father and I safaried into the little known regions of Northern Kenya in the little green Suzuki Jeep, with its canvas roof. The doors had been removed so we weren't quite so cramped. We would spend three weeks at a time, giving ourselves a chance to explore and enjoy these almost unknown territories. We would head north on these safaris around twice a year, so we learnt a lot about all the areas we visited. In those days there was no form of electronic communication, other than in towns or on some of the larger ranches, so nobody would be able to contact us once we had left for safari, and no one would have a clue where we were during those three weeks.

The Suzuki would be grossly overloaded, and it was just incredible how much we managed to carry: tools, spare wheels and inner tubes, spare parts, food and water for three weeks, and all our camping gear. Of course, there had to be room for some beers and homemade wine. We had Range Rover tyres fitted on the Suzuki, which gave it the ability to go almost anywhere.

Of course, one could replenish water supplies from the rare mission stations on occasion and also purchase a little fuel, if the missions happened to have any spare. Mostly we replenished our water from waterholes dug in the dry riverbeds by tribesmen: the Samburu tribe in the Milgis and Rendille or the Gabbra tribesmen, depending on the area. Sometimes we filled our water cans from Lake Turkana or the natural springs on the north side of the Chalbi Desert.

***

Our Suzuki safaris, we always had the intention of going farther into uninhabited and, to a great extent, unexplored areas of the vast Northern Frontier. On the 21st of September 1985, heading slowly north along a two-wheel track parallel with the immense bulk of the Mathews Range, we crossed the deep and dry Seiya River bed and made our camp for the night on its northern banks under the cool and dappled shade of the *acacia tortilis* trees. It was hot, and we cleared an area of fallen thorns that had deposited themselves under the trees, readying to set up camp. After unloading our camping gear, the next thing to do was put a pan of water on to boil for a mug of tea. We carried small gas cylinders and a single gas ring, so it made life simpler if we hadn't had a chance of to collect firewood before getting camp ready. Collecting up a few dry sticks around the camp areas was a small job that always had to be done, provided we were in a location where dry wood could be found. It was a delight to have a small fire burning in the evenings.

Our camps always became home no matter where we were. Having settled in, we relaxed in camp chairs, enjoying listening to the many species of bird calls, when we started to hear a faint, distant, deep roaring sound, which became louder—the sky to the west and the distant mountains were now a very dark, deep, bluish black. A gigantic storm had developed in the mountains above Maralal area. The roar continued to get deeper and louder.

Rising from our camp chairs, we walked to the edge of the *lugga* and clambered down onto the flat of the riverbed. There was nothing to be seen at that moment, but, while waiting and straining our eyes along the Seiya *lugga*, we saw that clouds of dust were forming, and behind the dust was an enormous torrent of rolling waves of water three to four feet deep coming towards us and picking up speed as it came! What an amazing sight, and my camera was left in my tent. No time to run and fetch it now.

Scampering back up the bank, we returned to camp and waited and watched. Moments later, there was a roaring, muddy crescendo of fast-moving water, around one-hundred-yards wide, completely filling the *lugga* from one bank to the other. The flash flood was now a swift flowing river, brown in colour from the surrounding silt it gathered along the way. The flow continued at speed, deep into the night. The distant thunder receded in intensity until all was silent, with just the hoot of an owl to be heard.

By dawn the following morning all the water had passed, leaving a treacherous-looking, muddy *lugga,* strewn with branches and tree trunks that had been wrenched from their roots upstream and brutally carried along with the rapid flow to be deposited and left abandoned in the riverbed. It would take a few days of bright sunshine to dry up the remaining mud, provided it didn't rain in the mountains again.

Our camp was still very dry, as the rain had not reached us. It had been many miles away up in the mountains. Packing up camp after a light breakfast, we left our Seiya *lugga* camp to continue our safari. There was still almost three weeks of adventure ahead.

During one of our many adventurous safaris, we reached the great Milgis *lugga.* It winds its way east from mountains and runoffs from the west between the Mathews and Ndoto ranges and ends its journey way out in the Kaisut Desert, some hundred or more miles from the source. It is a very strange and mysterious riverbed, at five hundred yards wide in places. It flows after heavy rains in the surrounding mountains. We would enter the Milgis at Barsaloi, a small outpost, and travel slowly along, stopping to camp on its high banks and explore the area, over a distance of around seventy miles, which would take several days, as the going is slow. The Milgis is a very interesting *lugga* and, at the time of our safaris, would have an abundance of wildlife: elephants, lions, reticulated giraffes, greater kudu and many other varieties of plains game, including Grey's zebra. The bird life is prolific; they live in the forests of acacia trees that grace the banks of the *lugga*.

Samburu and Rendille people dig deep wells within the Milgis for water for themselves and their livestock, including cattle, sheep, goats, and camels. Water flows gently along the surface of the great wide *lugga* in places, weaving its way eastwards in little rivulets that hug the banks, and then, depending on the terrain, trickles its way across to its centre, and then to its far bank. The water disappears underground for many miles, giving one a false sense of security, and then the water appears again. It will be totally dry, and then, suddenly, farther along, the water reaches the surface once more. It is like this for a great part of the year. When in full spate, it becomes an enormously dangerous torrent of gushing, rolling waves, five to six hundred yards wide, with whirlpools and undercurrents all swirling along. This only occurs when there are heavy rains in the surrounding mountains. During a normal dry season, the riverbed can be completely dry on the surface, but very wet underneath with a deceptively dry veneer on top. One can walk over the seemingly dry coating of sand that appears to be hard ground, but turning to retrace one's steps, one can see the ground trembling where one has just walked. Retracing ones steps is very hazardous, as the riverbed becomes a quicksand in just moments. Samburu and Rendille people have even lost their camels in the quicksand of the Milgis *lugga* on occasion.

On this particular safari, we were happily travelling along on what I can only describe as a dry surface, when suddenly and unknowingly, we obviously hit on a section of the *lugga* that was wet underneath. The little Suzuki sank dramatically up to its open doorways, coming to a grinding halt. Father stepped out from the driving seat on to hard ground, but when I stepped out, I immediately sank up to my thighs. What a terrifying and dramatic experience! Fortunately I was still holding on to the vehicle. Trying to pull myself out, there was a horrid sucking sound. Once in this dreadful muddy silt it is extremely difficult to get out. The damp sand underneath the dry surface was sucking me down, but, with great difficulty, I managed to pull myself out and back into the vehicle, getting out on the driver's side. Had I not been hanging on to part of the Suzuki with one hand and onto Father, who managed to remain on hard ground, with my other hand, I could have been sucked under so easily.

We were totally and utterly bogged down with no hope of just the two of us getting the vehicle out. There was roughly two hundred yards of riverbed on either side of us. While contemplating what in the world we were going to do, a group of six or seven young Samburu Moran came striding along the *lugga* from the Barsaloi direction. All were carrying spears and *simes* (long, thin double-edged knives) strapped to their waists on leather thongs, and dressed in the usual red cloth tied also around the waist, naked above but for coloured beads around their heads and necks.

They could hardly speak any Kiswahili, so communication by language was not easy, but hardly necessary as the situation was patently obvious. Father unloaded our shovel and *jembe* (hoe), and we began to try to dig the sticky, gluey mud from around the vehicle. The young men decided to help, and we all took turns digging. During the digging process, they all started chanting, just the way they do when digging one of their wells for water. It was an amazing sight to see all these young warriors singing and chanting while burrowing their way around the car—taking wet muddy sand from around it was one of the most unusual scenes that I have ever experienced.

Meanwhile, Father had cut some bush from the north bank of the *lugga* to place under the wheels to give them grip. Five hours later, in four-wheel drive and low ratio, we were able to drive out of the now deep hole and onto hard ground once again. Gifts of sugar, tea, and chewing tobacco were given to the men for their help, and they were all delighted. Some of them took to looking at themselves in the wing mirrors on the Suzuki, and there were peals of laughter from all—they had never seen their own reflections before. Most of these tribesmen knew little about money; hence, we gave sugar, tea, and tobacco to people in thanks for any help we received. By the evening, when we located a suitable place farther along the Milgis *lugga* to camp for the night, we were totally exhausted and covered from head to foot in Milgis mud.

The following morning, we regained our strength and dug a hole a few feet deep in the riverbed, and within an hour or two it had filled with wonderful, clear fresh water from the underground flow. We filled and replenished all of our cans and water bags, and then I sank my body into this marvellous bath. It was absolute bliss. I washed my sweaty, mud-caked hair and let it dry in the hot Northern Frontier winds. A half hour later, the bath cleared again, as fresh water came up through the sand at one side and seeped out the other. While I started packing up camp, Father enjoyed his bath, too, right in the middle of the Milgis *lugga*.

***

A year or so later, on an evening stroll along the Milgis a short distance from camp, we came upon lion spoor, deeply imprinted in the sand. The spoor looked to be a few hours old, and indicated possibly three or four lions heading in the same direction we were. We weren't too concerned. They would be ahead of us, and Father had the shotgun over his shoulder with S.S.G. ammunition in it. In this area of the Milgis, the elevation is around three thousand and five hundred feet above sea level and has a beautiful temperature in the evenings. Our shadows were very elongated as the sun sank over the hills in the west, giving an orange glow on the flat sandy *lugga* and providing for a perfect and peaceful walk.

Thank goodness I slept through it all, as at dawn the next morning, while enjoying a mug of steaming hot tea outside the tent, we spotted lion spoor all around our camp. The lions had walked everywhere and even stepped over the guy ropes of the tent, having walked round it several times. I dread to think what might have taken place had we been sleeping out under the stars and not under canvas!

One evening, camped ten miles or so up the Seiya *lugga*, I was sitting in my bush-green canvas chair gazing up at the vast range of mountains towering above. The Mathews Range stretches for seventy or eighty miles and runs approximately north and south. The banks of the Seiya, like the Milgis, are covered in vegetation, including groves of *acacia tortilis*, their branches spreading out like umbrellas, giving shade for the smaller plants. The greenery follows the water courses for hundreds of miles. Scanning the scenery on the opposite bank to where we were camped, we saw a large *acacia tortilis* covered in beautiful pink *ipomoea* flowers, a wild morning glory. This species was a creeper, and it covered a considerable area of the tree's shapely branches, cascading down towards the sandy ground.

I walked across the Seiya to the far bank with my camera, with the intention of photographing the delicate, colourful blooms. When I arrived at the foot of the tree and was admiring the scene, I instantly became aware of a strange feeling that danger was close. There was no particular reason that I could think of for this feeling of discomfort; however, I put my camera in its case and headed back to camp. Father asked if I had managed to get some good shots of the flowers. I explained my reason for retreating without spending time on the far side of the *lugga*.

The following morning while waiting for water to boil for tea, I wandered back to have another look as the blooms were beginning to open, and, to my shock and astonishment, the sand below the tree had enormous pug tracks of lion, which had not been there the previous evening. I wasted no time retracing my tracks back to camp. Needless to say, the flowers remained unphotographed. I can only assume that my mental telepathy was working overtime, and that I sensed danger from the lion, which must have been very close by.

***

On yet another safari driving along the Seiya *lugga*, we had located a delightful spot for camping high up on the Eastern Bank. Everything was set out, and the camp looked like home. I even made our evening meal. We were quite exhausted from the day's journey. Relaxing with a mug of Tusker lager, I enjoyed watching the evening sun sinking over the distant hills in the west. A few moments later, we heard the ominous sound of thunder in the east. Looking up into the heights of the Mathews Mountains, the sky appeared forbidding. It became very dark, thunder came closer by the minute, and then an enormous rainstorm developed.

We now had no alternative but to hastily dismantle our camp and bundle everything back into the Suzuki. Drinks and supper were abandoned, because we had to move out of the area as fast as possible. This was most disturbing, as now it was starting to get dark, and we needed to get out of the Seiya *lugga* before the rain running from the mountains formed rivers that flow into the *luggas*. In no time the *lugga* would flow, and we would be unable to get out. We were many miles from any roads or tracks, but several days of travelling into the wilderness, driving as fast as one can in a sandy riverbed, we made our way out of the area and reset up camp on the Northern Banks of the Milgis, where, at least, if both *luggas* started to flow with water, we could get out across country, if necessary. It was neither easy nor pleasant, setting up camp in the dark—the second time in one evening.

The Seiya can also be a very dangerous riverbed for quicksand. After it flows, it dries out on the surface but underneath can remain wet for many months. The damp, however, is not visible on the sandy exterior, so it is always advisable to only travel by vehicle along both the Seiya and Milgis *luggas* in the height of the dry season. Sometimes, though, one can get caught out in unseasonal rain in the mountains.

A neighbouring rancher once told us that, thirty years previously, he had been travelling in the Seiya, hit one of the quicksand areas and lost his Land Rover. It just sank through the surface and kept on sinking, out of sight forever, never to be seen again. He was very fortunate to have survived such a dreadful incident. To this day, his Land Rover remains under the sands of the Seiya *lugga*.

***

133

The Kaisut Desert is a vast area covered in sparse scrub bush; Baio Mountain and the Ndoto Range run along its southern region. The Kaisut has many attractive rocky outcrops and dry sandy riverbeds. Along the seasonal sand rivers grow some of the larger *acacia tortilis* trees, as they receive water when the sand rivers flow after the rain in the Ndoto Mountains.

Along the northern zones, before the Kaisut merges with the Karoli Desert, there are low-lying, granite, rocky outcrops, running in the direction from north to south throughout the country. One particular sand *lugga* runs its course amongst a number of these outcrops, where giant boulders appear to rise out of the white sandy surface. We would almost always camp in this location. There were several very large attractive *acacia tortilis* trees growing in the overflow part of the *lugga*, which was all whitish sand, giving wonderful shade, their branches spreading extensively, so we were able to park the vehicle and set up our entire camp under all-day shade.

Here we would always spend several days, affording time to relax and go for long walks to explore. Our camp would be left unattended, but the tent flaps closed, a padlock on, and any personal documents put in a bag and carried with us. We would walk or drive for hours; fortunately, there was never anybody, or very seldom anybody, in that area, mainly due to being a waterless area. Along the *luggas* there would be spurfowl and guinea fowl and the vulturine guinea fowl, which are good eating, so Father would shoot one or two so that we could enjoy a meal of fresh meat, not having had any for many days.

Back in camp, there was plenty of dried wood around the foot of the trees for making a fire on the sand. When there were enough hot ashes, Father would dig a shallow hole in the sand, put in a shovel-full of hot ash, a shovel of sand, and another of ash. This mixture was perfect for an outdoor oven. I would prepare the fowls, wrap the meat in foil, and place this in two tin *sufurias* (metal pots), one on top of the other. I would then bolt the pots together and place them in our oven, covering it over with sand and hot ash. The potatoes and onions were wrapped in foil and put in the hot coals of the open fire. When all was cooked, we ate a wonderful supper together with a mug of Father's homemade wine.

While our meal was cooking, a bottle of lager would be placed in a large, wet sock and hung up in a tree. The breeze blowing through the wet sock (kept especially for that purpose) helped to cool down the beer. Climbing to the top of the nearest outcrop of rocks with our mugs, the beer and some crisps, we would sit looking out over a fantastic arena of African wilderness that stretched for hundreds of miles, the mountain ranges in the distance all around us, and watch the sun slide down out of view over the distant horizon, while sipping our beers and nibbling crisps. Later, taking the *sufurias* out of our bush oven, we enjoyed a sumptuous meal all prepared outdoors. Sometimes dust managed to find its way into our food. It could be an extremely windy place.

Father was very good at making safari bread out in the bush. He would mix and knead the dough, place it in the *sufurias*, leave it to rise in the zipped up tent, so no breeze could get in, and then bake it in our bush oven. So long as he only left it for twenty minutes, it would turn out perfectly; if left any longer, it would turn out a black charred mass. He got it down to a fine art, and we enjoyed freshly baked bread with honey.

I had taken two bottles of my own homemade plum wine. We decided to bury them deep in a crevice on top of the outcrops of rocks where we had our sundowners. It was something I had done for fun, making sure they would never be found by any passing cattle or camel herders (not that the tribes spent time in the area—it was totally waterless). I planned to unearth the bottles on our next safari. We would have something fun to look forward to the next time we visited the Kaisut Desert, though we had no idea when that might be.

Eighteen months later, camped in that very same spot, which was our favourite place for spending a number of days, because it was very beautiful, wild, and peaceful, we went up onto the rocks and unearthed the bottles. I was in trepidation as to whether the corks would still be intact or whether ants may have burrowed their way through, but—lo and behold!—both bottles were intact. Wiping the dust away from one bottle, we opened it and enjoyed it with our evening meal. It was superb and nicely matured. The second bottle we kept, took it back home, and then on down to Mombasa to share with Mummy and Andrew.

In February 1985, one of the driest months, we were camped below the immensity of Baio Mountain. It stands alone towering above the Kaisut Desert. The heat and dust can be overpowering; it's a very dry heat without a vestige of humidity. High winds sweep the dust in billowing clouds across the arid and parched Kaisut, vegetation of whatever kind looking desiccated, and enormous granite boulders that must have rolled down from Baio thousands of years ago are strewn around and about. Our little camp was situated next to one massive boulder leaning over at an acute angle, so the ground beneath was in shade for much of the day. We just had early supper, the western sky deep pink and glowing onto the surrounding desert sand. In total peace we relaxed, enjoying our camp fire and drinking an evening mug of hot chocolate. In the far distance we noticed movement and saw the silhouette of people gliding along, arms swinging from side to side. The group changed direction, having detected us, and headed towards our camp. The group consisted of twenty Rendille women of varying ages, carrying small tin cans and other receptacles. They were dressed in longish garments made of goat hide tied on one shoulder and adorned with beads. They could not speak Swahili at all, but asked in sign language if they might spend the night next to us for fear of lions. We watched them collect up dry sticks and light four or five fires in a circle; why so many we had no idea. We gave them some tea leaves and sugar, and they carried their own limited amount of water in calabashes. As it became darker, the new moon appeared and the stars began to twinkling brightly. Each woman, in turn, started to walk round and round the enormous boulder. We couldn't understand this ritual. After walking round, each woman would sit on the ground by one of the small fires, and another woman would get up and parade round the rock, come back, and sit down again.

When all had completed the strange behaviour, they began melodic singing, a most unusual and enchanting melody of sound. Some of the women would chant quite loudly, and then the rest would echo in a softer tone. The light from the fires reflected onto the huge boulder and the contours of the women's faces and bodies, while the rest of their dark shapes merged and blended into the night. We watched this mystical vision in total awe and fascination. The women continued this ritual long after we had retired to our camp beds. They slept the night on the hard ground beside the big rock. At five in the morning, we heard faint sounds of movement. A few minutes later when we went out to watch dawn approach, we saw that the women had disappeared with no trace left, but for the remains of cold ash from their little fires. Like phantoms, they had arrived and departed. It all seemed so unreal and like an ethereal dream.

The Chalbi Desert is a very wild, bleak, and extremely windy area of Kenya's Northern Frontier District; the desert is actually an old lake bed and one of the hottest places I have ever been. At four o'clock in the afternoon, under the shade of beautiful doum palms, the temperature was 50 degrees Celsius, which means that the midday temperature is even hotter. On the northern side of the Chalbi there is a wall of black lava boulders, which stretch as far as the Ethiopian Border. Below the wall of hot lava are belts of the most beautiful doum palms growing out of fresh clear water which bubbles out of the ground in many places. The Chalbi is the home of the nomadic Gabbra tribe, a very attractive people who cross borders between Ethiopia and Kenya.

We had driven all the way along the Balesa *lugga,* which runs around seventy miles or more from the slopes of Mount Nyiru and the Ol-Donyo Mara ranges and joins up with tributaries from Mount Kulal. It ends its journey at the southern side of the Chalbi Desert, spreading out and mingling into the white sand dunes covering the southern side of the Chalbi.

We arrived at the dunes without having seen a vehicle track for many days. We just travelled across country with our maps and compass for guidance. The dunes are many hillocks, around ten to fifteen feet high, very close together, making driving through them difficult. Crossing one such dune, the Suzuki began to slide badly on the sand to the left side, so I was almost about to spill out through the open doorway. The car reached a critical angle and would have rolled over, but Father stopped the engine, and we very carefully stepped out of the Suzuki. Gently, we started to take the sand away from the two right-side wheels, and slowly the vehicle began to slip to a more level and favourable position. This was a touch and go situation, as, had the Suzuki rolled over, we would have been in a very critical situation. No other humans could be found in many, many miles. Having levelled the vehicle, we stepped back in and drove off the dune.

On another safari, we had driven off the salt pan of the Chalbi and into the dunes to explore. Parking the vehicle by one of many dunes, we got out to walk a short distance and climb a dune so we could see across the country. When we came to retrace our steps back to the car, the high winds, which reach eighty miles per hour, had, of course, blown sand over our footprints so we couldn't find the vehicle. There is not a single tree or bush in this territory, no shade whatsoever, just scorching sun, burning winds, and hundreds of dunes, all much the same shape and size. This situation was most unpleasant and very worrying; everywhere looked the same.

On the flat of the Chalbi is a salt crust, so tracks of a vehicle or camel remain very visible for as long as two years, as it hardly ever rains there. We walked back onto the desert, found our vehicle tracks, and followed them back into the dunes. Fortunately, there was still a faint trace of the wheel tracks, so we finally found our Suzuki.

In the centre of the Chalbi, is a sand dune roughly two miles long. It runs east to west and is approximately thirty feet high. It is difficult to climb, due to being very steep and slippery. Once on top, it immediately drops straight down the other side. There is just a narrow needle-point top, with no room to even stand before toppling over the other side. We had been searching for this particular sand dune for many years, but were unable to locate it until we came upon it by mistake, thinking it was the southern side of the desert. It was quite a shock to find, when we reached the top, that it was just a dune, and the lake bed of the desert carried on for miles beyond it.

The belt of green doum palms along the north side of the Chalbi Desert grows below a great lava flow of black boulders. Water bubbles out of the ground in places, so bright-green grass of a very spiky kind grows prolifically. The Gabbra people come in to water their camels at these springs, as well as a few cattle and goats. The stock also feeds on the grass that can grow several inches high overnight.

When the Gabbra return to southern Ethiopia after rain there, the Chalbi springs are left totally uninhabited and the grass grows up to ten feet tall, waving to and fro in the strong wind. The thousands of palm fronds rustle, making a terrific crescendo.

We were heading east along the Chalbi, after having spent several enchanting days in the springs' area. It was exceptionally hot as it always is, and the usual gale-force winds were as burning hot as ever, blowing at a rate of sixty to eighty miles per hour. The sky was blue and cloudless over towards the outpost of North Horr, some twenty five miles away, where there is a round-shaped hill that can be seen for many miles, as it stands alone in open desert. We noticed a small cloud forming around its top, and, happily continuing on our way, we did not think much about it. Within minutes, the cloud became larger, and, instead of being a white puff, it was turning dark, its appearance like that of an atomic bomb going off. It increased rapidly and became a huge storm cloud. Now we were beginning to get concerned, because, once it rains on the Chalbi, there is no getting out, as it becomes a dangerous sea of boggy salt-pan mud. Even camels become bogged down and cannot get up and die on occasion. The Suzuki was grinding along as fast as possible, which was not fast. Even when dry, wheels of any vehicle sink two to three inches into and through the salt-crust of the lakebed silt, so going is hard.

To the north was now a gigantic sandstorm, at least ten miles across, coming straight for us at a speed of what must have been sixty or more miles an hour and, behind it, a most vicious rain storm. There was no getting out of this! With no time left, the sandstorm was upon us and hit us broadside, rocking the vehicle violently. All the Chalbi dirt came in through the open doorways covering us and everything in the car. The high gale-force wind and dust made it impossible for us to see or hear anything. We were hardly moving. Then the rainstorm hit us, the heavy rain drops stinging our faces, arms, and the uncovered parts of our legs, soaking us to the skin and turning the thick deposit of Chalbi silt into a horrendous, gluey mud. The wheels of the vehicle were getting caked up, too, thicker and thicker until we were almost at a standstill.

Looking out through the open doorway, I spotted an area of what looked to be hard, rocky ground, and we quickly turned left onto it. Thank goodness it was hard ground. Coming to a stop and switching off the engine, we sat looking out into a blur of heavy rain, feeling cold, wet and miserable. After an hour or so, the storm passed. We unloaded all of our equipment and laid it out on the hard surface to try and dry it out. What an absolute mess we and all our belongings were in. Horrendous!

We managed to erect the tent. At least the sleeping bags were clean, wrapped in bags. Later towards evening, a young Gabbra boy came along with a dozen or so camels. He had come from his home off from the Chalbi a few miles where the ground was sandier with scrub bush. He indicated that there would be absolutely no possible way we would be able to get out of the area by way of the Chalbi; it was just a sea of treacherous mud. There were no roads at all for many miles. We were in the middle of nowhere. The young boy offered to show us a way out across country and would come to our camp in the morning.

The Gabbra boy of about fifteen years of age arrived just as we completed loading up and scraping the mud off the tyres. He squeezed himself into the car beside me, which only had two small seats, and pointed to the way we should head out. The terrain was extremely rough, and we drove in and out of gullies, over rocks, mounds of earth, and scrub bush. I thought we would never come to the end of this rough and most uncomfortable ride.

Five exhausting hours later, we came upon the track from North Horr to Loiyangalani, an outpost on the shores of Lake Turkana. It was still half a day's journey to reach the lake, and the track was very rough and rocky. The nice young boy was delighted to be given two hundred shillings and, with a broad smile showing perfect white teeth, said he was very happy to walk all those miles back to his camels and home. We were so relieved to be on a reasonably drivable track and eventually reached the shores of Lake Turkana. The Jade Sea crocodiles glide up and down in the water just off shore, but we found a rocky part where the crocs find it too difficult to get into and cleaned up all our camping equipment and enjoyed a lovely lake bath.

***

Nine months later, our vehicle tracks were still visible on the Chalbi! Nobody had ventured in that area at all, which shows how wild that area is.

There are some springs on the southwest side of the Chalbi where the Gabbra people make water troughs out of clay from which their camels drink. It is the kind of earth surrounding that spring area that is wonderfully smooth and pliable. I collected some of this amazing clay to bring home and, after sieving it, I made decorative small vases as ornaments and painted them in varying designs.

There were a number of Gabbra families at the springs as we arrived. They were shy but gracious. One young woman came up to us with her beautiful little baby of about eight months old, who gazed at us with big brown eyes. The child had somehow fallen into the fire and burnt one arm very badly. The mother asked if we could help. A good remedy for burns is bicarbonate of soda. We mixed a paste of thick bicarb with a little water, plastered it over the baby's burnt arm, and bound it up with a bandage. To my utter surprise, the poor little baby never made a murmur. The mother would then have to walk forty miles across country through the desert to the nearest mission station, which was at North Horr.

Susan M. Hall

Driving along the Chalbi one morning, we spotted camel trails leading south off from the desert towards Mount Kulal. We decided to follow them in the vehicle, just as a matter of interest, to see where and how far they went. After travelling slowly across country and along the camel paths for many hours, we came upon a spring bubbling out of the ground and surrounded by the usual doum palms that grow in those northern areas. There were a number of families, again of the Gabbra tribe, spread out with many camels, all there for the water. On seeing us arrive, the women rushed off into hiding. The men looked in utter astonishment. One old man with a white beard, turban, and wearing the usual off-white attire typical of the Gabbra men, came up to us. He could speak a little Swahili and asked how we could possibly have arrived there. As he said, only donkeys, camels, and people on foot could reach this wild place. He also assured us that *we* were the first white people ever to reach that spring. The people from this area had, of course, seen white people at the far-off mission station, but never had a white man or woman been to this area before. The old man had lived there all his life and was amazed that this Suzuki Jeep could manage to get there. He asked if we could please exchange the Jeep with him for two donkeys.

Travelling along the Balesa Kulal *lugga*—a very soft, sandy *lugga* and easy to become bogged down in the dry, whitish sand—we came upon six or seven Gabbra men digging a well within the riverbed. They had not heard us approach, as they were at different levels down the well, digging and passing the sand up to the next man and on to the next to throw out. Stopping to see what was going on, we wandered over to where they were working and looked down into the well. The men were totally naked and looked up in complete horror and surprise. They were extremely embarrassed, so I moved away. They came out of the well, one by one, and dashed to find their garments to cover their nakedness. There was one very good looking man around forty-five years old with a fine face, high cheek bones, and fine lips. He had a neat, white beard and moustache and wore the usual turban; long, strangely fitting, off-white shorts; and a white shawl or cape over one shoulder. I asked him if he would mind if I photographed him. He said, "Definitely not." My friends would see the photos of him and all laugh! Poor man. I put my camera away, and he noticeably relaxed. Then we had a long conversation with him.

The Gabbra people were definitely the most attractive and gracious people I had ever come across.

Safaris in the North

Kenya's northern deserts beckon and pull like a magnet to which I am irresistibly drawn. Here I find peace and solitude, which pervades.
— Thelma G. Hall

There were tall, quivering, dark shapes wobbling about in the sky and totally unrecognisable—a mirage in the Chalbi Desert, wave motions of visual fallacy. Sometimes there are round shapes floating that, when we get closer, turn out to be a tiny conglomerate of lava stones or a small hill, giving the appearance of two flying saucers. Shapes in the lower sky looking like a forest of trees are, in fact, one small bush less than two feet tall. Other, taller spirally shapes reflecting in "water," is really a camel train crossing the Chalbi. No water exists at all; the nearest lake is a day's drive away. Even the people seem to be visions floating in the sky. These are all remarkable mirages, which I have managed to capture with my camera. The Chalbi Desert is the only place where I have experienced such visions. The midday heat is like a furnace, which is when mirages are most impressive.

If one is driving with the wind, one cannot get enough speed to out run it, so the vehicle will boil in no time at all, because no breeze is blowing into the radiator. Once, our battery actually melted on top when the heat was so tremendous. The high gale-force winds are baking hot, much like a furnace. One longs for the wind to stop so one can cool down, but it never does. It is relentless, day and night. Even at night there is still a hot wind coming off the black lava boulders and the Chalbi itself. Such are the conditions in the Chalbi desert.

Climbing the Mountains

Ol-Lolokwe

Ol-Lolokwe, or Oldonyo Sabach, is the first large mountain of merit that I climbed with Father. In appearance, it is an enormous, flat-topped mountain rising up alone just south of the Mathews Range. Very impressive, it is a stunning feature with a vast granite cliff face north of Samburu and Shaba Game Reserves.

My parents and I were staying at Samburu Lodge, the first lodge to ever be built on the banks of the Euaso Nyeru River. We always admired the surrounding mountains and Ol-Lolokwe in particular.

I was around twenty-two years old at the time, and we decided, since we were staying at the lodge twenty-five miles or so away from Ol-Lolokwe, it would be a lovely idea for Daddy and me to go climbing and hopefully reach the top. Mummy would relax at the lodge until our return. We left the lodge early in the morning and drove to the base of Ol-Lolokwe. Looking up, I found it rather forbidding, its huge cliffs towering up into the sky. The hot sun beat down, and there was little wind, if any. It was all thick bush. We were scrambling in and out of thorny bush to begin with, and there were some difficult cliffs to negotiate. Finding elephant and rhino tracks to follow made it easier, as they follow the contours of the mountain sides. In those days, very few people, if any, ever got to climb Ol-Lolokwe; however, one of my gentlemen friends at the time, a game warden for Samburu and Laikipia Districts who came to live in Kenya from the UK, had climbed it from the north side. We ascended from the east side.

Susan M. Hall

It was fairly hard going. As we got closer to the summit, there was a variety of interesting plants. Apart from the wild fig trees, there are the amazing cycads, a variety that we had not seen anywhere else. The vegetation became greener, a contrast from the dry, scrub bush lower down.

Close to the top, there is water on the surface where elephants and rhinos drink. It is incredible that they climb all that way, when the Euaso River is not far away. The attraction is, no doubt, the greener vegetation for feeding.

The country surrounding Ol-Lolokwe is two thousand and seven hundred feet above sea level. I would estimate the top of the mountain to be around seven thousand feet. It was very wild and beautiful, with extensive views to the north: Baio Mountain in the far distance, the closer Mathews range, and Mount Kenya way to the south. We drank from the pool of water, but it proved not to be such a good idea, as later I discovered that I had picked up amoebic dysentery.

Quite possibly in those days there wasn't even a Mountain Club of Kenya, at least we hadn't heard about it, but years later we heard that the mountain club used to scale Ol-Lolokwe and a manmade path had appeared. There was no such path when Father and I went to explore this vast mountain, just elephant and rhino trails.

We followed the same game trails back down and returned to Samburu Lodge, having enjoyed a most successful day. We were back with Mummy, and the three of us enjoyed a lovely evening together. I was enthralled that we had achieved this climb, and it gave me an appetite for exploring more of the mountains in northern Kenya.

Baio

Baio emerges out of the Kaisut Desert like a wave evolves in the ocean. It is shaped like a wave about to break; anyway, that is the way I see it. On numerous safaris, we could be parked under the sparse shade of a tortilis tree to have a simple light lunch, usually of biscuits, tinned tomatoes, and dates. For many years I gazed up at Baio, with longing to one day reach its summit. At the very top is a rock that juts out beyond the rest of the mountain. From the ground it looks like a thin needle protruding out into the air. From that needle point overhanging the bulk of the mountain, the drop straight down is approximately six thousand feet. It had been my constant wish to get to the top of that needle-shaped point.

Finally the day came, when on one of our adventurous safaris in October 1981, Father and I decided to climb Baio.

Camping at the base of the northern side, we dug a substantial depression in the ground to bury fuel, water, food, and personal belongings, as we didn't have a lockup vehicle—the Suzuki remained open, as the canvas doors had been removed so as not to be cramped inside. At five in the morning, we had a quick bowl of oats and tinned milk, buried our belongings, covered everything with sand, and then drove the vehicle over the top of our "underground" safe. We could not be sure that tribesmen, who may come past, would not steal our belongings. Having set off with gun, cameras, and water bottles, we headed up through thick, thorny, dry scrub-bush. The "wait a bit" thorns on the bushes clung to and ripped our clothes as well as our skin, and the ground's shaley, loose stones slid beneath our feet. The climb was difficult, but not dangerous, if one was careful. We crossed over steep valleys and ravines that took us way down before going up again. It was quite exhausting. Fortunately, as we got higher, it became misty, which cooled the air.

We followed rhino trails for a large part of the way up. When we finally reached what we imagined was the top, we found ourselves in thick moisture, a wet mist. Initially it was extremely disappointing, because there was no view whatsoever. We were surrounded by damp clouds swirling around us. The vegetation on the top was amazing; there appears to be plants that are not seen anywhere else. While studying the plant life, the mist suddenly cleared, giving us the most breath-taking views of wildest Africa. There is not an extensive area on top of Baio, and on reaching the edge of the mountain, one sees a most dramatic drop of six thousand feet to the bottom. Now, what looked like a needle protruding out when we were on the ground, turned out to be an enormous slab of granite rock jutting out away from the edge of the mountain. The winds on the top were tremendous swirling round the cliffs, and many swallows were flying around, zooming back and forth at high speed. Did we dare to go up onto that slab of rock jutting straight out into space? Yes, but one of us at a time climbed up on hands and knees, in order not to get blown off the top—a six-thousand-foot drop! I stood up momentarily, and Father took a photo of me on the top, and then I came down and Father went up for the experience, and I photographed him on the top. We were taking a risk, as the swirling winds kept gusting and changing direction. There was no way that one could remain in a standing position for more than a few seconds, before having to sit down quickly and hang on to the surface of the rock. I named that jutting-out piece of rock "Lover's Leap." Looking down and south from the top, we spotted a lake—incredible to see in the desert country. We never realized water was there, but now we understood where the rhinos went to drink and why in the past, we had seen pelicans flying over the Kaisut. We slowly and carefully made our way back down this incredible mountain, slipping and sliding on the steep terrain. Seeing our tiny camp at the bottom, it looked like a lifetime away—a speck on the landscape, all alone in the vastness of the Kaisut. It appeared to take us forever to travel up and down the extensive valleys. Finally, we made it back to camp. It had been a nine-hour journey up and down.

***

Months later, on a safari to explore other places, we made a point of finding the lake we had seen from the top of Baio. That lake is an overflow from the Milgis *lugga* and is seasonal. It's called Larapasi and is several miles long and accommodates a profusion of bird life, including pelicans. Mud fish live in Larapasi. They hibernate under the mud when the lake dries out on top.

Camped on the water's edge, we were able to have luxurious baths and replenish our water supply. An especially nice Samburu man came into camp from some distance away. He was most concerned about our safety from lions, because several of his tribe had been taken and eaten, he said. He kindly offered us his spear, for which we thanked him very much, and, in return, we showed him our shotgun. He went away satisfied for our safety.

Poi

On every safari that takes us along the Ndoto Range, the most prominent mountain one sees is Poi. It stands out as a mountain on its own, although it is part of the extensive Ndoto Range. It is an enormous bulk of granite cliff face. The Kaisut Desert flanking the north side of the Ndotos is roughly two thousand and five hundred feet above sea level. The top of Poi is in the region of eight thousand and five hundred feet. This was another great mountain I always had wanted to climb to the top of. The local Samburu and Ndorobo "honey hunters" always told us that nobody could possibly reach the top. They had taken cattle part way up some of the steep slopes of most of the mountains, and the honey hunters had been to the top of most of the mountains, but not to the top of Poi. This made it even more exciting for me. I was more determined than ever to attempt to try to get to the top. But how?

There were attempts by professionals from all parts of the world to get to the top by climbing the cliff face with ropes, but, by all accounts, from what the local tribesmen had told us, nobody actually managed to get to the top by that time. Some climbers had got part way, and some had ended up falling to their deaths. Various missionaries we had come to know who worked in the Ndoto area knew this, and had told us as much. One honey hunter by the name of Locual, a Ndorobo man, said he had collected honey on all the mountains, but had only been part way up Poi. "It is just not possible," he told us.

I suggested to Father that we fly from home across to the Ndotos in the Navion, so as to fly round the top of Poi and look for a way up. Besides the three- to four-thousand-foot cliff-faces, we, not being mountain climbers, obviously would never be able to think of a way on our own. We flew around on many occasions and came to a decision on which area of the mountain we would attempt, if we ever got the courage and the chance.

Several missionary families worked up north, including one American family who lived at Ngurunit, a small outpost tucked under the shadows of the Ndotos. We had become friendly with them, and they used to visit us at Enasoit when they were on their way to Nairobi. While staying with us on one of their excursions to civilisation, I asked Dale if we could possibly leave all our camping gear at their place while we attempted to climb Poi. He and his wife said that would be fine and invited us to stay with them over that period, which would make things much easier for us. I asked Dale if he would join us. At first he said, "No." He had been part way up Poi and would never attempt it again. Later, he had second thoughts and said he thought he would come with us, provided we really would attempt to reach the top. We would ask Locusal, the Ndorobo honey hunter, to come with us.

A month later, Mother went with Andrew by train to Mombasa to spend some time with him, while Father and I packed the Suzuki for another safari. Having travelled around most of our chosen areas, we left the Poi climb to almost the end of the safari. A day or two before, we camped by the rocks at our favourite sand river in the Kaisut and shot and cooked a couple of vulturine guinea fowls in our bush oven, the hole in the sand having been dug the day before, so we could build up our strength for the climb.

While staying with the mission friends at Ngurunit the night before climbing, we met Locusal, who agreed to come with us but told us we would never make it to the top. Nobody ever had, so he said. We prepared ourselves the evening before. I packed dates for us to eat—they are an amazing source of energy, particularly when one is not eating anything else—filled our water bottles, put film in the camera, and picked up the gun all ready.

The three of us were up at four in the morning. We had a bowl of mixed dried fruit and oats with milk—difficult for me to eat at that time of morning. I was extremely excited about and somewhat frightened of what to expect. When we got into Dale's open Jeep, it was still very dark. We collected Loculal from the Samburu boma and headed off towards the base of Poi, travelling along a rocky and sandy tributary, which flows when there is rain on the mountain. The going was exceedingly difficult, as there was soft sand and large boulders to negotiate. Parking the Jeep where it would be in shade from an overhanging tree, we started walking towards the base of Poi, stumbling over rocks and sliding in the sand as the Eastern sky began to pale. It was a three-mile walk before we even started to ascend the bulk of the mountain.

Loculal had lived at Ngurunit near Poi all his life, and, as we walked, he said that he had been up all the mountains in the area to find honey, which he sold to his people as well as to the missionaries. He had only been part way up Poi and told us that it was not going to be possible to reach the top or anywhere near the top of this huge and formidable mountain. He, however, was quite willing to see how far we could get.

It was very steep right from the start. There was a thick forest in the first gorge we entered and especially steep with enormous boulders. Loculal cut thin poles from branches of trees for us to use for leverage and stability.

The gorges on Poi are thick with canopies of wild fig trees and many other species, and the water gushes down in torrents during heavy rain on the mountain. I had to hang on to trunks of trees to pull myself up, as did the menfolk, due to the steepness of the terrain we were scrambling up. Our water bottles swayed back and forth, as did my camera. When we came to sheer cliff faces, Loculal cut long vines that hung from the forest trees. He managed to get himself up, and then threw down one end of the long vine. So, one at a time, we hung on to the vine while Loculal grasped the other end and helped to haul us up the cliffs.

This situation took place on many occasions all the way up the steep gorge areas and cliff faces. The vines were amazingly strong and supported our weight without breaking. It was not without fear that I negotiated the cliff faces. We had never done rope climbing in our lives, but the vines gave enough support to negotiate these impossible cliffs, provided one end didn't slip out of Loculal's hands or our hands. On we went, up and up, stopping, from time to time, for a mouthful of water from our bottles and a few dates for energy. It was certainly becoming extremely challenging, but I was *so* determined to reach the top of Poi that nothing would stop me.

We arrived at a more level and grassy plateau, which Dale reckoned was the top, but I told him that this was absolutely *not* the top. I knew very well from our previous flights around the top what the terrain should look like, and we were still a long way from the top. After having a rest stop, I went on ahead, leaving the men to follow. Father was a short distance behind me, and the other two some way back. Now we came to a horribly difficult situation: a thousand feet of scree rock rising almost straight up. We had come to an even more dangerous—and what looked to be impossible—climb for us. I wondered how on earth we would ever get back down, but for the time being, all I wanted to do was reach the top of Poi, come what may!

Crawling on hands and knees much of the way up this thousand-foot chunk of steep granite scree was very taxing on our limbs. We could hardly stand up when we reached the grassy slope at the top of a huge steep area. We walked through a grassy area interspersed with juniper trees for what must have been half a mile or more. I was still ahead of the men and finally came to a flat rocky platform, which was indeed the top of Poi. There was a dramatic sheer drop over the edge, straight down approximately six and a half thousand feet to the bottom country! The men came up behind me, and we looked over the edge in absolute awe. No one can ever know just how I felt at having reached the top of this magnificent mountain. Nothing else seemed to matter anymore, at that moment … nothing at all! I was just so exhilarated and had achieved the ultimate, something I wanted to do for many years.

The views were unbelievably spectacular. We were truly on top of the world. I just couldn't believe we had actually made it to the top of this most dangerous and deadly mountain. Loculal could not believe it either! We rested up there on the top, and I took photos and just admired the dramatic scene. It was like being up in an aircraft. We were above the cloud level, the clouds little puffs of cumulous. We looked all that way down to what appeared to be tiny threads of sand *luggas* so far down. The thought of even attempting to head all that way back down didn't bear thinking about.

Having enjoyed relaxing for a short time at the top, we headed back along the grassy plateau to the horrifying thousand feet of slippery granite-rock-part of the mountain side. Pieces of shale dislodged under our feet and the strain on one's knees was tremendous, with the incline being so severe. I felt my right knee give suddenly, and the pain was excruciating. There was still eight hundred feet to the bottom of that section of the mountain, and another six thousand feet beyond that to the surrounding country below. Now that my knee had let me down, I could hardly operate my right leg. I tried sitting on my bottom and sliding, inch by inch, but trying to hang on to tiny plants growing out of the rock was not helpful at all, as the plants came away in my hands. The plants were just surviving on the surface of the rock from the morning dew. We dared not speak or say a word, each of us concentrating on *not* slipping. One false move and there would be no recovering one's grip. One would roll all the way, gaining momentum, to the bottom of that part of the mountain. This mountain was all but impossible to negotiate and extremely dangerous.

That region of the mountain completed, we continued down. I was suffering badly with my knee. We used the same vines that Locual had cut on our way up and the same system to get down the cliff faces, now more difficult for me with a damaged knee. Of course, we could not retrace our steps on exactly the same route, the mountain being so extensive with granite cliffs all looking similar. Trying to negotiate one such cliff face became absolutely horrendous. Locual managed to get himself from one side of the cliff, which was twelve to fifteen feet across, to the other, his long arms and legs reaching out for hand holds and foot holds—tiny ledges on the otherwise smooth rock face. We could see there was no way I could possibly reach and hold on to the little ledges of rock.

Dale got into a position on the edge of the cliff face with his stretched-out hands holding onto tiny ledges no wider than two inches, placed his feet at right angles on similar ledges, and held his body close to the rock. Next, I had to ease myself between Dale and the rock face. Father held my right hand, but had to let go as I got out of his reach. I placed my feet on top of Dale's heavy boots and my hands on his arms. There was a two-thousand-foot drop to the forest below us. I couldn't reach far enough to my left where Loculal had his hand outstretched trying to reach me. Dale said, "Don't look down. Just ease to the left." I froze with terror. If Dale slipped with my weight on his feet, we would both crash down the two thousand feet to the forest below.

I was totally numb with fear. I couldn't get back to Father, and I couldn't reach Loculal. We were stuck. Father was suffering desperate uneasiness at our predicament, but unable to assist in any way; he just couldn't reach. Dale and I were in the middle of this cliff face. It would only be moments before he would slip. I tried to reach out to Loculal, who was hanging stretched out across the edge to try and reach my hand …

I don't know how it happened, but I suddenly found myself attached to Loculal. I was now across the cliff and onto solid ground. My head was whirling, and I was bathed in perspiration. Dale managed to reach the little ledges and ease himself across, and then Father, being very agile, managed to reach out and cling to the tiny ledges of rock and get across to us. That terrible fright had taken the stuffing right out of me. I felt weak and useless at that point. I just could not believe that we had not fallen off that cliff face to our deaths.

Father and I had finished our water, and I could feel my throat drying out and burning from exhaustion. I felt desperately thirsty. Dale had got Loculal to carry a larger bottle for himself, but Father and I had run out. Loculal and his people, having lived in the desert for centuries and, with ebony-coloured skin, could take the sun and dry heat much better than we pale-skinned people could. Loculal never touched a drop of water the entire day, until he was home. We continued to ease our way down the great mountainside, my thirst becoming unbearable.

Down, down, and still down, it seemed to take forever to reach the sand *lugga* at the bottom, and, by now, it was almost dark. Tripping over rocks and sliding in the sand, we made our way along the *lugga* to Dale's Jeep. I was *so* relieved, but when we got in the Jeep, it refused to start, so Father and I had to start pushing it through thick sand. As if we were not exhausted enough! Finally, we got it started and eased along the *lugga*, past large boulders and over small bushes for several miles with the headlights on, until we came to the track leading back to the mission station and the house. It was eight in the evening, and we had been on Poi for fourteen hours.

Dale's wife was worried that we had suffered an accident, which we very nearly had. We desperately needed to drink, and she gave us all a cold mug of Coca-Cola, which we gulped down thirstily. That was a big mistake. As I drank, my throat seized up totally and became extremely painful. I should have asked for room-temperature water and not attempted to drink cold Coca-Cola. Having been so desperately thirsty, I had trouble with my throat for a number of days after, which prevented me from eating properly. It was getting towards the end of our very successful safari. Four days later we reached home.

Having spent two days checking on the ranch and cleaning up all the camping equipment for storing away, to be ready for the next safari, Father and I drove down to Mombasa in the Range Rover to meet up and be with Mother and Andrew. When the Mountain Club of Kenya heard through friends of ours involved with the club that we had climbed to the top of Poi, they contacted us and wanted to know which route we had taken, how long it had taken, had we climbed with ropes, etc. We gave them as much information as we could, having discussed this with us. Some while later, four professional, overseas climbers and four amateurs decided to follow the instructions of how *we* had reached the top of Poi. They all decided to attempt the climb the following Easter.

155

On their return they contacted us again. They had made it to the top, having gone the same route we had, but only just managed with great difficulty, and having used ropes. They could not understand how *we* had managed it. They said to us, "We are professional mountaineers, and we had awful difficulties. You are not climbers at all, so how in the world you managed it, we can't understand."

I had never felt so proud. Unfortunately, my knee was damaged for life, so my serious climbing days were over.

The Ndotos

The day after climbing Poi, Father and I went for a day's walk following the stream flowing down from the mountains above Ngurunit, all part of the Ndotos. It is a very beautiful stream cascading over large and small rounded boulders, with a variety of magnificent trees and shrubs growing along its banks. Wandering along, sometimes in the cool water, and then along the banks, we followed the stream way up into the mountain gorge. It was not a strenuous ascent; we sauntered along slowly, enjoying the sound of the water as it rolled its way down, clear and sparkling in the sunshine, with cool shade from the lush green vegetation. Little waterfalls here and there made the area perfectly charming. We wore light clothing as always when on safari. Feeling hot, we just sat under one of the shallow bubbling waterfalls to get cool. The hot sun dried us completely in minutes. That day was delightfully relaxing. We headed back down to the mission house later in the afternoon.

The Navion Rangemaster, on take-off

My late brother Andrew

Susan M. Hall

Mt. Nyeru, Horr Valley, North Kenya

Gabra people, with camels, moving through the Chalbi desert, in a mirage

158

Camels in the Chalbi, in a heat haze

Gabra people, with loaded camels, crossing the Chalbi desert, the "Huri Hills" in Ethiopia in the distance

Susan M. Hall

Me (Susan) sitting in the Milgis dry river bed

Father (John) sitting in our camp, at Karawi springs, Chalbi

Doum palms, swaying in the wind, Karawi springs

PART THREE
AIRCRAFT DAYS

THE AIRCRAFT WE OWNED

*Fly high among the fluffy clouds, enjoy the tranquil peace; I
can tell you my secrets aloud with no-one else to hear.*
— Susan M. Hall

The Piper Cruiser

The first aircraft we owned during mid to late 1950s was
a single engine Piper Cruiser, fabric covered, registration
number VP-KFS. It was a three-seater: the pilot seat in front
and a bench seat for two behind. Even though my mother was
very slim with a slight build, and Andrew and I were small children, the four of us fitted into the Cruiser snugly. I remember
while I was at Nakuru Boarding School and all the children
were on the playing field, Father would sometimes fly over low.
"Susan, your Dad is coming!" the other children would cry out.
We would wave madly, and I would feel so proud. My parents
were the only parents of all the school children who owned an
aircraft.

During some of the school holidays we would fly from
Lanet Airstrip outside of Nakuru to Wilson Aerodrome to refuel,
and then on to Malindi, a four-hour flight in the little Cruiser.
On arrival, we would circle low over the Blue Marlin Hotel,
and the manager would drive out to the airfield to collect us
and our small amount of luggage and take us back to the Hotel.
We never had to book rooms in those days, because there was
always space available. We always planned to stay five or six
holiday days there. It cost all of Ksh 30 per day per room, with
full board. The English manager and his wife had two sons:
one was my age and the younger boy was Andrew's age. I was
around ten or eleven years old and became good friends with

the elder boy. After a wonderful day on the beach, we would get ourselves all smartened up, and he would invite me for a drink at the bar: lemonade or Coca-Cola. His parents agreed to let us youngsters sit at the bar when it was early, before the adults came for their sundowners and dinner. The boy, Dave, was an expert at surfing the waves without a surfboard and, of course, showing off to me. He could also climb to the top of coconut palm trees just like the local Arab boys. He and I became very good friends and even wrote to one another from school for a year or two. We lost touch after he, his parents, and brother left Kenya for somewhere in Southern Africa.

On our holidays at the beach in Malindi, our parents would hire a little *Mini-Moke* to go on drives along the coast and around Malindi. Long walks on the Malindi Bay Beach were a delight. We swam and surfed in the huge fifteen-foot waves; the sea rolled in right up to the hotel walls. There was often an Arab man, Mohamud Said, on the beach. He walked up and down calling in at the four hotels to try and sell his trinkets: Arab silver bracelets, copper trays, and other attractive jewellery. He was nearly always the only other person on the beach in Malindi Bay and would come up to us with his trinkets wrapped up in newspaper, taking great pains to open each silver piece. We bought silverware from him from time to time over the years.

Before leaving the hotel to fly home, Andrew and I would always draw an enormous picture on the clean, tan-coloured sand, and then ask Father if we could fly low over it so we could view our drawing from the air. Oh, such fun!

The First Beechcraft Bonanza, VP-KHU

When Father was thinking of selling the Piper Cruiser, we went all around Wilson Aerodrome looking at various aircraft. Mother and Father knew a man on the airfield who mentioned that he had a very nice Beechcraft Bonanza for sale. It belonged to a man from Kitali, so we went along to have a look at it. Dull orange and white in colour and a poor paint design, it was parked outside the hanger. It was a V-tailed Bonanza.

She looked rather shabby, and Father was not too impressed. Keith, the owner of the company, said to Father, "John, I will repaint this Bonanza for you, free of charge, if you would like to buy it."

Father replied, "Well, Keith, I don't think we can afford it at the moment."

Keith told Father that once it was repainted, Father would not be able to resist it. We all walked away laughing.

Sometime later when we went back, we saw outside Keith's workshop and hanger the most stunning looking aircraft we had ever seen. It was a sleek, V-tailed Bonanza painted red and white with black trim and a paint design doing it real justice. Now, a "princess" of all aircraft, we were all intoxicated by the sheer beauty of this aeroplane. The engineer had known just how to paint this aircraft in order to attract Father and, indeed, all of us. He knew that it would be totally irresistible.

We were living on Nderit Estate at Lake Nakuru at the time, when the beautiful VP-KHU Bonanza became part of our family. She was a fast single-engine aeroplane. Now, it only took us two and a half hours to fly to Malindi for our coast holidays. A luxurious four-seater with upholstery like a small airliner, she was royal amongst light aircraft. When we moved to Enasoit Ranch from Nderit Estate, a hanger was erected, and VP-KHU was flown by Father to her new home. It was but a few months later when poor workmanship on the Certificate of Airworthiness caused us to suffer the tragic accident (mentioned earlier), which was the end of our beautiful Bonanza. It was a complete write-off.

The Second Beechcraft Bonanza, VP-KGU

For our business of cattle trading, we needed an aircraft, so just under a year later when another Bonanza came up for sale Father bought it. We talked about having her painted the same red and white, but decided against it. It just didn't feel right, so we had her painted blue and white instead. She was still very smart looking, just not as regal. For some unknown reason, she

167

didn't seem to fly quite as fast as KHU, not a significant difference though.

The Bonanza is not a bush aircraft. She takes a longer run to get off the ground than some light aircraft, as she is not designed for grass or bush airfields, so we took extra care on ranch airstrips. Unlike the Piper Cruiser, which has a fixed undercarriage, the Bonanza has an electrically operated retractable under carriage. It is also single control, not duel control.

My father had given me all the books on how to learn to fly, which I went through with great interest. After studying everything, Father decided it was time I tried the practical: flying the aircraft. On one of our flights out on cattle business, Father did just that—he handed the controls to me. Being a single control, one has to unlatch a pin, pull it out, and move the controls from the left-hand pilot seat over to the right-hand co-pilot seat in order for the co-pilot to be able to fly the Bonanza. I was fifteen years old, and this was my first attempt at actually flying the plane, keeping it straight and level. I managed this all right, although I felt a little nervous, it being a single control, as I was in total control of the aircraft. We did this often, until I was completely comfortable with it, and then Father started to teach me to do turns. Unfortunately, I was not able to learn take-offs and landings in the Bonanza, due to its single control unit. The landings and take-offs came later when we owned the Navion Rangemaster.

We were on a flight from Nairobi back home one day after collecting the plane from its annual Certificate of Airworthiness (C of A) inspection when smoke started to appear from the cowling area. This was most disconcerting. Was the engine on fire? Fortunately, we were not far from home, and after landing, Father opened the bonnet and found two oily rags left lying on the engine by the engineers who had worked on the service of the plane. The plane could have caught on fire while we were flying! Collecting up the burnt cloths, Father put them into a bag, and the next time we flew to Wilson Aerodrome, he dumped them on the desk in front of the engineers, which drew some very guilty looks and mumbles of apology.

I was sixteen when Father and our friend, Nigel, decided that the four of us should do a safari by air in the Bonanza and fly from Enasoit to South Africa to visit Nigel's sister and husband, who lived outside Johannesburg. It was a long way in a light aircraft, with Father flying and Nigel in the front with him, and Mother and I in the back. We took off from Enasoit, spent a night at the aero club, refuelled at Wilson, and set off. Our first stop was Mbeya in Tanzania to refuel. The grass runway at Mbeya was very short with tall trees at each end. We were heavy with fuel, full tanks, ourselves, and our luggage. We got off the ground all right, as Father kept the nose down to gain speed and pulled up over the trees, but it wasn't the best of situations for taking off with a load. A heading was set for Salisbury (in what was at that time Southern Rhodesia), a four-hour flight from Mbeya. We spent the night at Meekles, a hotel in Salisbury (now Harare), a rather smart and expensive place. I remember walking down the street in the evening to look for a restaurant for supper. In the morning when we went to breakfast, not only were the menfolk expected to wear jacket and tie for dinner, which was a very rea-sonable idea, but they were expected to do so for breakfast, too! Father and Nigel had not brought jackets and ties, so we were sent to the children's dining room for breakfast.

We flew from Salisbury to Pietersburg in South Africa where we had to clear customs, and then on to Johannesburg. It was two long days of flying in a small aircraft.

Several days later, we flew down to Durban, borrowed a car from Nigel's mother, and drove to the Drakensberg Mountains, where we stayed in a quaint little hotel called Champagne Cas-tle. During the few days we spent there, it rained quite heavily, but we were able to go for walks in the mountains. The four of us drove back to Durban and, after a day looking around the town, flew back to Johannesburg. Two days flying to Nairobi and the following day we got back home, overall a remarkable flight in our four-seater Bonanza. In October of 1966, the blue and white Bonanza was sold to a neighbouring rancher. Father was interested in buying a different kind of aircraft called a Navion Rangemaster.

Susan M. Hall

The First Navion Rangemaster, N2500T, 5Y-AFM

Mother and I stayed in a house at Watamu Beach as Father
had gone to the USA to have a look at a Navion Rangemaster
aircraft. While enjoying the creamy sands of Watamu Beach, we
would drive into Malindi town for shopping and go for walks in
Malindi Bay on the golden-brown beach sparkling with mica.
The beach was dark in colour from the silt being washed down
hundreds of miles along the Galana-Sabaki River. Mother and
I became very suntanned over the two weeks we were at the
coast.

When Father returned, we were terribly excited to hear that
he had, indeed, bought the Navion he had been to see and fly
while he was in Texas. Father asked Mother and me to guess the
colour of the lovely new aircraft, and we guessed every colour
under the sun, but it wasn't any of the usual colours. It was a
brilliant gold and white with burnt-orange and black trim. We
just couldn't wait for this aircraft to come over from Texas. It
was the demonstration model for the Navion Company. A ferry
pilot was to fly it all the way from the United States to Nairobi.
Oh, how excited we all were.

On our way back to the ranch, we stopped off in Nairobi to
see my brother, Andrew, and give him the delightful news. He
was thrilled. Now, we all waited in anticipation. On arrival, the
ferry pilot flew the Navion into JKA, the main airport in Nairobi. The aircraft had to be cleared through customs there. We
drove out to the airport to meet up with the ferry pilot, Hans.
Initially, we couldn't see the Navion amongst all the huge Boe-
ing and other airliners, and then we spotted the beautiful gold
wonder parked under the wing of some enormous passenger aircraft. Several days later, Hans flew the Navion up to the ranch
and spent a few days with us.

Standing alone now, the Navion looked marvellous, regal,
and beautiful, with the sun glinting on her brilliant gold wings.
She looked like a star standing there in the African wilderness.
She arrived with an American registration N2500T, but later it
was changed to a Kenyan registration 5Y-AFM.

The Rangemaster is a five seater, the seats with armrests. Ours had beautiful upholstery in orange check, the leather areas in black. She was like a little airliner. The aircraft was used for all our cattle-trading business, and I learnt to do my take-offs and landings in the Navion, being dual control. After a while I could fly the Navion with confidence and did so often.

In February 1967, we were visiting a farm in the Timau area looking at some very nice cattle to purchase. There were three of us in the plane: Father, my cousin David, and myself, with David in front with Father. Just after take-off, the engine cut out; the wheels were already up in their wheel housing. There was little time to think what to do: turn to the right into the low country and hope the engine would start, knowing if it didn't, we would be forced to land in rough and rocky country or turn to the left and come down in a grass field. It seems that there was an air lock in the fuel system and not enough time to put on the electric booster pump and, without power from the engine, no electrics were working.

The sun was glinting on the Navion's beautiful gold wings as we came down and hit the ground with a considerable bump and skidded along on the belly of the aircraft. The propeller, hitting the ground and cutting into the grass, became severely damaged, and the seat belts cut into our thighs with the impact. We climbed out, after coming to a grinding halt, somewhat stunned. The damage didn't look too bad, apart from the fuselage being buckled underneath and the propeller, of course. The owner of the farm had seen what had happened and come straight over in his vehicle. He was as shocked as we were at the unfortunate incident. We all decided that if we jacked up the plane, pumped the wheels down manually, and fitted a new propeller, Father could probably fly the plane out of the field and get it to Nairobi to be repaired. The suggestion was that we lift the tilted wing and support it with bales of hay until we could get a new propeller brought in and fitted, and then jack up the plane to get the undercarriage down. The farm owner organized his workers to bring in the bales of hay, and we secured the aircraft so that it was level. We were then kindly driven all the way back home to Enasoit where Mother was waiting for us, not having a clue what had happened, and desperately worried.

Another disaster took place with the aircraft that night. Cattle got into that particular field, found the bales of hay supporting the plane, and proceeded to eat the hay. In doing so, they trampled all over the wings, denting them very badly, and totally and utterly damaging the aircraft beyond belief. This was a horrendous and disastrous situation. Our beautiful gold Navion, which Father had bought only a few months before, was a complete write-off. It had to be dismantled and taken to Nairobi on two lorries, where companies on Wilson Aerodrome refused to take it in, because my father was the agent for Navon in Kenya. They said, "You are the agent, you sort it out!" The companies were all very jealous. They wanted the agency for Navion, and so would not help in any way.

A very kind and decent man in the police air-wing hangar agreed to unload the wreck and put it on one side of his hangar until we could plan who would rebuild the Navion. The companies on Wilson Airport refused to rebuild our plane, just because Father was given the agency by the Navion Society in Texas. Father was the only person in Kenya to own a Navion, but because they were not given the agency, they refused to help. Things transpired, and the next step was that the plane was finally flown to Addis Ababa in two aircraft: a VC10 and a Dakota. It was to be rebuilt there, which took fourteen months.

When the Navion was finally flown back to Nairobi from Addis Ababa, we found the repaint job to be a disaster. They had not managed to mix the paint to the original gold, so it had turned out more a dull brown. It was so very disappointing. No one on Wilson Aerodrome got the gold colour mix correct; they tried but just couldn't get it right. I designed a whole new colour scheme, as we did not want a brown plane. We had it totally repainted in turquoise and white with black trim. It was not, by any means, as startling to look at as the original gold, but a lot nicer than miserable brown. It was so terribly disappointing to have lost that stunning gold that it had arrived in from Texas.

I would often take over the flying when we were on cattle-buying trips. I desperately wanted to get my pilot's licence, but, no matter how many hours one had flown, it was still mandatory to have fifty hours under professional instruction, which neither my parents nor I could afford. It was very expensive—one had to pay by the hour—so it didn't happen, to my great disappointment. It was very different when Father got his licence—all the hours he had flown were counted in for the fifty hours—but by the time it was my turn, the flying laws had changed to one having to obtain fifty hours with a qualified instructor, no matter how many hours of flying experience one had.

We would all fly from Enasoit to the coast for holidays, where my grandmother had an eight-acre plot of land at Watamu, and where we had, at one time, had a house built for her. The closest landing ground was Malindi, about fourteen miles from the Watamu property. After flying low over the house, my grandmother would drive out to collect us. Many years later, friends who also lived along Watamu Beach, would come out to the airport to pick us up.

I had a little Maltese terrier, no bigger than a toy, and the little, white, fluffy pet used to love flying with us. He was always first into the plane, straight into the pilot seat, where he waited expectantly for us all to get in before settling down for take-off. He would sleep most of the way, as we would fly at an altitude of fourteen thousand feet above sea level. Woopsie, as he was named, would groggily get up from time to time and look out of the windows to see if we had arrived. When we landed, Woopsie would get terribly excited because he couldn't wait to get out to see and smell what interesting things there might be out there, and he couldn't wait to get to the beach. It was only a two-hour flight from Enasoit Ranch to Malindi in the Navion.

We owned a small boat with an outboard engine, which was kept at the house. It didn't take us long to get it out and into the water whenever we stayed at the Watamu house. I remember the wonderful idyllic days going out in our boat to explore Mida Creek or go snorkelling in the coral gardens out in the ocean and seeing all the beautiful-coloured little fish swimming around the pretty coral. We would spend all morning out with the boat, sometimes taking a picnic lunch out to Whale Island near the mouth of Mida Creek where we could wallow in the coral pools when the tide was low or sit on the small area of sandy beach. We would be the only people there on the tiny island, so private and totally relaxing. It was imperative that we left this idyllic place to get back to shore before the tide came back in. The sea could become very rough with huge waves around Whale Island and the Mida Creek area, where, at spring tides, the ocean flows in and out of the creek at a speed of around thirty miles per hour with an incredibly strong and dangerous current.

One day when Father and I were out snorkelling a short distance south of the Mida Creek mouth, I was suddenly badly stung all down my left side and became paralyzed on that side, making it almost impossible for me to swim back to the boat. Fortunately, Father was close by and, although not being a good swimmer himself, managed to drag me through the water back to the boat, where I had difficulty climbing in. There were big red welts all down my left side where I had been stung. After getting back into the boat, we noticed many colourless jellyfish floating about—it was obviously one of these that had stung me. We had not noticed them while we were snorkelling. After about twenty minutes, the pain decreased, and the ugly red swollen welts slowly faded as I recovered.

There were a number of times when we had trouble with the boat engine. On occasion the sheer pin would break, and it would be an impossible situation for us to row the boat against the spring tides around Mida Creek, and we were carried out away from shore several times. Having our house close to Mida Creek meant that we almost always went boating in that area. The bird life up the creek was fantastic, and we often went by boat to watch birds come in at sundown, particularly at neap tides. At spring tides, one could expect very turbulent seas close to the creek. It was exhausting trying to get the boat back home in these conditions, particularly on the occasions when the engine failed. It was only a six-horse power engine, which was no match for the severe tides coming in and out of Mida Creek.

We did have a lot of fun in the clear turquoise waters out from our house at that time. The beach hardly ever had anyone else on it, and we would walk for miles along the cream-coloured sandy Watamu Beach, enjoying the sea breeze and sunshine.

After having collected the plane from its annual check-up, Father, Andrew, and I were coming in to land at a neighbouring ranch a few days later. We checked the three green lights on the dashboard, indicating that the undercarriage was down and locked in position, but, as we touched down, the front wheel shot back into the wheel housing. We did a nose dive along the grass airstrip, dust billowing up in clouds as the propeller churned up the ground. The aircraft came to a halt fairly quickly as, fortunately, the airstrip was uphill. It was a frightening shock to all three of us. The front of the plane was obviously badly damaged and the propeller completely twisted up. The accident meant two problems had happened, mistakes made by the engineers who worked for the company where we had the maintenance done: First, all three green lights came on and the red danger-light went out as usual, indicating all wheels were down and locked, when, actually, the front one was not. Secondly, why didn't the front wheel lock into place as it should have done? This meant that the engineers who worked on the aircraft had overtightened some parts in the front wheel strut, and the lights in the cabin, indicating the position of the undercarriage, had not been synchronized correctly. This could have caused the three of us to be severely hurt or worse, but landing uphill saved us from doing a summersault in the aircraft. The company paid for the repairs but *not* for the spare parts, which had to come from the USA. This company should have taken full responsibility, but people do tend to get out of doing so.

We had 5Y-AFM for many years, flying all over the country for our cattle-trading business. There came a time when business was slow, so there was not too much use for the aircraft, and it became expensive to keep as it still had to be maintained, costing more than our business could manage at that time. So, very sadly, our beautiful Navion, which had become so much part of our lives, had to be sold. It was the only Navion Rangemaster in Kenya.

175

The Second Navion Rangemaster N2486T, 5Y-BKL

Sometime later after business picked up, it was decided that we needed an aircraft again. Father contacted the Navion Society in Texas to enquire what Navions were for sale. Father had come to personally know the chairman of the Navion Society, and he sent a number of photographs with all the details of various Navion aircraft for sale. We chose one that looked to be suitable for us, but by the time they received Father's letter confirming that we would take it, that particular one had been sold. Another came up for sale, however, and Father secured it by sending a deposit.

A ferry pilot was organized to fly the plane over to Kenya for us. He was from Ireland, and ferrying aircraft from the USA to various parts of the world was his business. The money was sent over to the USA for the ferry pilot's fee and extra for whatever might be needed for the journey. In due course, the aircraft was fitted out with equipment for the long flight and an extra fuel tank installed inside the aircraft. The fuel tanks in the wings, together with the large wingtip tanks, enabled the Navion Rangemaster to fly for eighteen hundred miles, a range which is a considerable distance for a single-engine, light aircraft, but it needed the extra tank fitted for the long distances and extra safety between refuelling. We were informed of the date that the Navion would be leaving the USA for its long flight across the world. There would be overnight stops where the ferry pilot would rest and refuel the aircraft.

After around four days we were informed that the Navion reached Lagos in West Africa. Then we heard no more: it seemed that the aircraft was seized at Lagos Airport and impounded and the pilot arrested and put in jail! Now, we were in for big problems. We had absolutely no idea why the pilot would have been arrested and the aircraft impounded; there was most certainly some strange business going on. Then we heard that the pilot bribed his way out and got himself back to Ireland, leaving the aircraft in Lagos. The money he used to bribe the officials was Father's money! Father spent months trying to get the plane released. We could only assume that the ferry pilot was carrying some illegal goods, but had no way of finding out and never did get to know the truth.

The US Embassy in Nairobi tried everything to try to get our aircraft released. Months went by, and now we neither had the aircraft nor the money. Finally, Father decided to hire a pilot from around Wilson Aerodrome to go over and try to get our plane out of Lagos and to Nairobi. Nobody wanted the job; everyone said that it was too dangerous to fly the six hours over the dense forests of West Africa in a single-engine plane. Of course, a ferry pilot would be used to a flight like that. It needed an experienced pilot with a full instrument rating, but even the experienced pilots refused the flight. Yes, indeed, it needed a ferry pilot, but there wasn't one to be found at Wilson. Father would have liked to have gone himself, but didn't have an instrument rating. The plane had been sitting at Lagos Airport for months with nobody to check on it, a real worry.

Eventually, a lady pilot we knew offered to go over to Lagos to try and get the plane released and fly it back to Nairobi. She had a full instrument rating and, indeed, more grit than any of the men we had spoken to. She said she would need a qualified engineer to accompany her, and then she would be very willing to go. So it happened that she asked an engineer friend to go along, and they both went to Lagos by passenger airliner to try and get the Navion released.

This was all costing us an awful lot of money. When the two of them arrived in Lagos, they found the Navion parked in a corner of the airport and asked the authorities for permission to have it checked over so that they could fly it out in safety. The authorities at the airport refused permission to have the aircraft checked. They told the pilots to take the plane as it was now or not at all. What a horrible and risky situation! The pilots had no choice but to take the plane in whatever condition it happened to be in. They took off, after doing what checks they could, only to find a problem when they went to retract the undercarriage. It would not retract, but they could not return and land as the authorities would have refused to have checks done, and the aircraft would be grounded again, so the pilots had no alternative but to fly with the wheels down, causing drag on their speed and using up precious fuel. They decided to set a course and fly to Bangui, in the Central African Republic, in the hopes of finding help to repair the damage that the aircraft suffered while left at the airport in Lagos. The authorities at the airport, it seems, had dragged the plane along, probably towing it by its front wheel instead of with its own towing handle, doing untold damage. It was a long flight across to Bangui, where the two pilots managed to get a certain amount of repair work done on the undercarriage, and finally they flew in to Nairobi. A rough experience for the two pilots, they were paid handsomely for their fine efforts. Engineers at Wilson Airport checked the plane over, confirming that it was now in a satisfactory condition.

The aircraft looked very smart and attractive painted in burnt orange and white with a navy blue trimming. Father flew it back home to the ranch, and for the first few flights, take-offs and landings we did, it seemed to be absolutely all right.

Several weeks later, Mother and I were sitting in the patio area at our big Enasoit house one morning as Father headed off in the Navion to visit a nearby ranch. Mother and I heard the aircraft engine start up, saw the plane taxi out of sight along the airstrip, heard the engine checks being done and then the full throttle for take-off. The next moment, Mummy and I heard the most terrible bang, and then total silence. Quite obviously something terrible had happened. I dashed into the house for my car keys, and we drove at speed down the airstrip. There we saw the Navion tipped up on its nose, propeller in the ground, the tail way up in the air, and the entire nose wheel about thirty yards or so away to the left of the aircraft. It had snapped clean off as the plane built up speed for take-off. The arm of the nose wheel snapped off completely, putting the plane on its nose, but first grinding along for a short distance before coming to an abrupt halt. Father opened the door. He was still sitting in his seat, somewhat dazed but not hurt. This was an appalling situation, which could have caused an even worse accident, all due to what had taken place in Lagos. The engineers had not seen the problem in the arm of the front wheel, either in Bangui or at Wilson airport, so we had all thought that it was perfectly safe.

The following day, a friend came to visit us and, obviously, was very shocked to see the Navion on its nose on the airfield. He and Father managed to lay the front of the plane onto the back of our friend's Toyota pickup and tow the plane back to the hangar. We arranged for a pilot and an engineer to come up from Nairobi with a new propeller and, after fitting it, the pilot actually flew the aircraft to Wilson Airport for repairs. We were fortunate that the damage was not as bad as we had originally thought, but still a very costly business.

After getting over that unfortunate situation, we never had any trouble with our Navion Rangemaster. She was used for our continued cattle-trading business, flights to the coast, and shopping trips to Nairobi. We would visit other ranches to see friends. She arrived with registration N2486T from the USA and, of course, that had to be changed to the Kenyan registration of 5Y-BKL. Having got used to flying the first Navion, BKL was almost exactly the same, and I flew her often with Father on our cattle-buying expeditions.

After we sold Enasoit Ranch, there was nowhere close by to keep our aircraft, so eventually she had to be sold. It was a most heart-breaking experience, to say the least. It was the end of our aircraft ownership and the end of our flying days, forever.

Susan M. Hall

Father (John) in the Chalbi dunes

The Chalbi desert dunes

180

The Summit of "Baio"

Me (Susan) on the summit of "Baio"

Me (Susan) preparing wild Guinea Fowl, in the Kaisut desert

Father and Me (John and Susan) on the summit of "Poi"

From the summit of "Poi," looking over the Kaisut desert

The mountain of "Poi," in the Ndoto range, Kaisut desert

Me (Susan)

Keith and me, our wedding day, 2nd September 2000

Part Four
The Family

My Mother and Father, Thelma and John

My mother was born in Great Yarmouth, Norfolk, England. She enjoyed a very pleasant young life with her parents and time spent at the beach in a world of love and happiness until the Second World War broke out, and then disaster struck.

Mother and her younger sister had to be evacuated from their home in Norfolk and, fortunately for them, went to a lovely farm in the Tollerton area, outside Nottingham, to live with a Scottish family who had a delightful home and were very good to the two young girls. They were, of course, far away from their parents, which was very upsetting for the family. Mother's parents very sadly, had both passed away at a young age, all due to those harsh and miserable war years. Mother was only fourteen at the time of the great disaster. The two girls went to a day school close by. Later, Mother continued to live at the farm and worked hard with the Scottish family.

My father was born in Gunthorp, Nottinghamshire. Later, his family moved to Tollerton where my grandfather owned a small aerodrome and a number of fabric-covered aircraft, and he trained people to fly. Father worked on various farms in the area during his teens. The Hall family lived in a bungalow opposite the aerodrome at one end of Tollerton, and my Mother, from the Love family, now lived on the farm with the Scottish family at the other end of Tollerton.

Father with some of his friends, and Mother with friends of hers, inevitably met up along Tollerton Lane from time to time, so there would be a small group of youngsters who all got to know one another and become friends when they were all teenagers. As time went by, Mother and Father started to meet up

189

and go out on their own, and became very well known to one another.

As a young woman, my mother was a little shorter than average height and very slim with long, rich, black hair that hung in ringlets round her shoulders. She was a shy and particularly beautiful young woman.

Father was of average height, slim and strong, with fair, blond hair bleached by the summer sun while working in the hay fields. He owned a white horse and would ride along Tollerton Lane to visit my Mother, who would lean over the garden wall and wait in anticipation for him to come into view, looking out for the only rider coming along on his white horse.

Sometime later, the Halls leased two farms between Calverton and Oxton Villages outside Nottingham, which Father went to run. Mother and Father married and moved onto the farms: first, into an old three-storey house at Lodge Farm, where I was born, and then to Forest Farm house, a mile farther along the lane. Father always wanted to go to the wilds of Africa, and when things did not turn out well on the farms due to unforeseen conditions, Father applied for a job in Kenya.

In January 1953, when I was four and a half years old, my parents sold all their household goods and said good-bye to family and friends, and the three of us left England for good and came to Kenya.

In August later that year, my brother Andrew was born.

ANDREW, MY BROTHER

A Poem for Andrew from Me, Your Loving Sister

Old Zanzibar calls to me,
As we sail along on the sea
Towards the jewel of the African coast.
Oh Zanzibar Oh Zanzibar!
With your spiced coffee and tea.
Here we come, my friend and I
Looking for the treasures to buy!
Our friendly merchant is there with a smile
A cunning but pleasant man of style,
To greet us with spiced black coffee
And sweet Arab toffee;
Mr Ramya by name!
Here we come, my friend and I
Looking for treasures to buy!
We wander through old Narrow Streets
Searching for wooden antiques,
Or maybe brass pots, or old copper trays
Our interests run so many ways.
Here we come my friend and I
Looking for treasures to buy!
Or even a chandelier
But Oh! Do I fear!
For it is crystal;
If we slipped in the street
It would crash at our feet,
What a tragedy that would be!
Here we come my friend and I
Looking for treasures to buy!

191

Prince Amyn Aga Khan
Says he'll buy of my treasures, Ah Ha!
If I wait so much longer
For Prince Amyn to pass by my door,
I vow I'll sell him much more!
Here we come my friend and I
Looking for treasures to buy!
We load up the ship
With the help of our porters
While watched by their
Pretty, elegant daughters
Here we come my friend and I
Looking for treasures to buy!
Our ship is now loaded
So off we must go!
Back to Mombasa
The home we both know.
Until next time we come from afar
To visit Old Zanzibar!
Off we go my friend and I
Treasures all bought
So now, it's Goodbye!

—Susan M. Hall, July 1989

Andrew, my brother, was born on 6 August 1953 in Nakuru Hospital. I remember being taken to see the new-born baby and thinking what a perfect tiny person he was, with beautiful soft, rosy cheeks like a peach. As mentioned earlier, we all lived in the Wanjohi Valley (Happy Valley) at the time.

As Andrew grew out of babyhood, he loved to amuse himself, and later he and I would play together happily. We both loved being out of doors and would play for hours in the garden. He had a very gentle nature and loved to watch butterflies and other small creatures outside.

Much later, while I was in Nakuru Primary School, Andrew, at six years old, came for a short time to the same school. The girls' dormitories were quite a distance from the boys' dormitories, and Andrew, having been so used to being with me, could not understand why I was seemingly miles away from where he was although we were in the same school. He used to leave to come and look for me. Poor little boy, he was lonely and we always had been together at home. He just could not understand why he should be separated from me now. It was heart-breaking that we had to be kept apart at school.

When Nakuru Primary School became a girls' high school, Andrew had to leave. He was now sent to Nairobi Primary School, so we were months apart during school time. After primary school, Andrew went to Prince of Wales School, also in Nairobi, which he did not like at all and became quite ill with stress. My parents moved him to Coldhams Tutorial College, where he was a day student and went to live with friends. He became so much happier, as we all were to see him doing well.

During his time at Coldhams, he met the owner of a mining company who also owned a jeweller's shop called Elton's in Nairobi in the centre of the city. This gentleman offered Andrew a job to go all over Kenya and run various gemstone mines. Andrew was very keen on gemstones and was so delighted; it was a chance to get out of Nairobi, too. So, at sixteen years old, he left the tutorial college to take the job.

Andrew loved the life outdoors and being in wild areas mining beautiful gems. On occasion, his boss brought him back to Nairobi to work at the jeweller's shop, but he much preferred being out at the mines. He had sixty men working under him, so he had to be very strong willed to cope, being so young. The men adored Andrew, however, and he had very little trouble, if any, getting his men to work hard. While working on and around the various mines, Andrew and his workers were searching in the Tsavo area, when Andrew discovered the green garnet known later as tsavorite. Having found this green garnet, Andrew took samples back to his boss in Nairobi. His boss was so impressed; the depth of colour was just perfect. The company started to mine the area where the garnets were discovered and produced some of the world's most perfect green garnets, their colour the best ever produced, as was their quality.

Apart from mining the green garnets or tsavorites, they also mined rubies at Kasigau close to the Tanzanian border, and sapphires at Garbatula in Northeast Kenya. Unfortunately, the sapphires were not of the best colour or quality, so they concentrated on the tsavorite mine.

The boss of the company sent Andrew to Idar-Oberstein in Germany for three months' intensive training on how to cut gemstones. The tutors found him to be an absolute natural; he picked up the skill very quickly. After returning to Nairobi, Andrew started to do all the cutting of the best quality gems for sale in the shop. They employed a jeweller who made up beautiful pieces of jewellery.

Sadly, many years later, the gemstone company was sold, as Andrew's boss, the owner, left Kenya for South Africa. Andrew carried on working for the new owners but found them to be rather difficult and unsound in the gemstone business, so he decided to leave the company. Andrew and his lady friend at the time made plans to leave Nairobi, so they set up a rented home in the Old Town of Mombasa. His lady friend ran a restaurant on Wasini Island, and Andrew took out professional safaris around Kenya for a while.

There was a time when Andrew joined up with the crew of a ninety-two-foot schooner, sailing around many parts of the Indian Ocean trading goods. He loved his time on the sailing boat. He was away for three to four months on the schooner Sofia and came home with thick, long hair and a very attractive beard that had turned reddish colour from the saltwater and sun. I could hardly believe my eyes when he first arrived home. He was suntanned and slim, which made him look even taller. He was an extremely good looking man — no wonder all the ladies were after him!

Andrew was a very talented artist. He painted the most romantic seascapes in watercolour while living close to the ocean. We used to go out painting together when he was home and spend the most wonderful days outdoors, painting the scenes, talking and laughing. It was magic.

194

While living in the Old Town of Mombasa, Andrew decided to try the antique dealing business and bought up amazing furniture, some of it that had belonged to the Sultan of Zanzibar before the 1964 revolution. All the Sultan's furniture and his wonderful belongings were looted from his palace during the revolution when he had to flee to England.

Andrew went through all the shops and back rooms where all the artefacts and furniture had been left to rot in the damp heat of the Zanzibar climate over a period of twenty-five years. Andrew felt that he just had to try and save these beautiful things. He also bought up a lot of the brass and copper ware, again stored in the back of the Old Stone Town shops. Andrew hired a number of sailing boats and crew of people he had met in the Old Harbour at Mombasa to bring all the antiques, brass and copper ware, crystal chandeliers, and other items back from Zanzibar to Mombasa, where he worked repairing all the damaged goods and getting them back to their original quality.

Andrew tried hard to contact the Sultan, to assure him that a lot of his treasures were now saved. But, unfortunately, he was unable to make contact with him, so finally started to sell some of the pieces to hotels around Mombasa and along the coast. Now at least, some of the furniture had been saved and not left to rot in the back of those musty, damp rooms in the back of tiny shops in Zanzibar.

During the years that Andrew was trading in antiques between Zanzibar and Lamu, he bought a four-storey house in the Old Stone Town in Zanzibar. Most unfortunately, and very sadly, he never got the chance to live in it. He became very sick, and it was discovered that he had galloping sarcoma—an extremely rare cancer—in his pelvic bone.

The people of Mombasa and Zanzibar were very fond of Andrew and, when he would arrive by sailing boat to the shores of Zanzibar, the people would stand on the sea wall waving frantically and calling "*Tangawisi*," his nickname amongst the Arab and Swahili people. Tangawisi means ginger in Swahili, and was given to Andrew due to the fact that his hair and beard shone reddish or ginger-colour in the bright sunlight as he approached. His white gown and kikoi would blow in the coastal winds as the people of Zanzibar greeted him warmly, always ready to help load up the antiques, brass and copper ware, and chandeliers or whatever else was to be transport by sailing boast to Mombasa.

Andrew's illness was appalling, and he was in terrible pain, which put him and us through the greatest misery that I can remember. He passed away on the 5th of November 1991 in Nairobi Hospital.

To this day, twenty-four years later, he is missed so terribly by me and my parents. He is so well remembered and missed by the local people of Old Town Mombasa and Zanzibar. Andrew's art gallery in the Old Town of Mombasa was called Gallery Mashallah. To this day, it carries the same name and is a carpet and antique gallery.

Part Five
Life as an Artist

How It All Began

A profound love of the African wild;
Birds, animals, camel trains floating
Above the desert;
All have inspired me to capture it in
The timelessness of paint on canvas, in the
Exotic colours of nature:
Which has taught me so much
                                        —Thelma G. Hall

One morning, at the age of fifteen years, I was sitting on a carpet on the floor painting a picture of an African bird from a photograph when our friend and neighbour, Helen Myers, called to see us. She was intrigued by my first paintings and showed great interest in them, to my surprise and delight.

After returning back home, she told her husband, Ray, about the paintings she had seen and that same afternoon he drove over from their ranch, which bordered Enasoit, to see us, and he asked to see my paintings.

I never had any instruction in art or painting, it was just inspiration. Ray was impressed with my work and asked on the spot if he could buy two of the bird paintings. He paid me twenty shillings each. Twenty shillings was a considerable sum in those early days of the 1960s. The next time we saw Ray, he asked if I could paint twelve more bird pictures for him to make up a set for their home. This I did during my spare time when not working outside on the ranch. It was the beginning of my art career.

A short while later, after people saw the paintings Ray had bought, I began to get the odd commission from people we knew in and around Nanyuki. I was amazed and started to become very interested in painting birds of Kenya in watercolours. As time passed, I improved on the quality of my work. I happened to be in a framer's shop in Nairobi one day and by chance the well-known artist Rena Fennessy walked in. When we met she asked who painted the eagle picture that I was choosing a frame for, and I told her that it was my work. She replied, "Well, you will go a long way if you continue to paint like that!"

I was delighted and a little overwhelmed. All my paintings at that time were birds in watercolour. Later I started to paint other subjects, but the galleries in Nairobi preferred to hang my bird paintings for sale.

During the early 1970s, I took five bird paintings to London to the Tryon Art Gallery. I met the Honourable Tryon, who kindly hung my paintings in a beautiful room in his gallery next to the famous British bird artist Basil Ede's paintings. I was absolutely awed to have my work hanging in the Tryon Art Gallery in London. The paintings were not sold, as the Honourable Tryon said that people there expect to buy English birds not African, but he commended me on the detail and quality of my work.

In October 1978, my brother Andrew and I held an exhibition in the New Stanley Hotel in Nairobi. The exhibition was opened by the Speaker of Parliament at that time. It was very successful: we sold around 75 percent or our work. I painted many other subjects besides birds, which people liked, particularly my wildlife scenes. Andrew also painted a variety of subjects, including lovely paintings of ships and ocean scenes. Between us, we had a very attractive show of art.

Many people from various parts of the world visited our exhibition, including the well-known singer Helen Shapiro, who was visiting Kenya to sing at the Stanley Hotel. She came to the gallery to see our work. It was such a joy to have the opportunity of meeting and talking with her.

During the weeks of our exhibition, a man came in who wanted to buy a certain painting of buffalo in the sunset, but it already had a red sticker on, meaning that it was sold. The man was from Europe and carried a large briefcase. He was insistent on having that particular picture, but I explained to him that it was not possible for him to buy it as it already had been sold, but that I could paint something similar for him. "No," he said. "I want that one."

"Sorry," I replied. "You cannot have that one."

He went out of the gallery with a very sly expression on his face. The next morning, when we arrived at the gallery that painting was gone off the wall. It had been stolen!

The ornithologist, John G Williams, asked me to paint for his *Field Guide* books, which taught me even more about all the birds I painted. I worked very hard for over three years, painting over two hundred birds for a field guide book written by Williams. We were also working on several flower books, including *Flowers of East Africa*, which entailed a lot of travelling around Kenya to collect flower specimens for identification and painting. We were also working on *Orchids of Europe*.

My bird paintings were sent to Collins Publishers who published John G. Williams's previous field guides. Sir William Collins was delighted with my bird paintings and my designing of the plates for the book. He showed them to Sir Peter Scott, who wrote a lovely letter to me congratulating me on my work and saying how much he was looking forward to seeing the book in print.

After doing years of work for John G. Williams, I asked for some advanced payment, as I needed income, but he flatly refused, asking me to wait until the books were published, which I was not able to do—it meant that I had to spend more of my time on my own paintings for sale in order to create income. I just couldn't manage to paint for John G. Williams for twelve hours per day, which I had been doing, and not receive any payment for my work.

I wrote to Sir William Collins telling him of my predicament, as he was expecting all my work to continue to be sent to the publishers. He didn't know that I had not received a single cent over the three years. He wrote a very nice letter back to me, agreeing entirely, telling me to continue with my own work in order to create some income, if John G. Williams refused to pay me anything. Sadly, the books we were working on for those three years were never published. Collins Publishers refused to continue with John G. Williams, and he had to go and find another publisher. I did get all my bird plates back, having painted over two hundred birds, *and* I managed to sell some of the plates.

Sir William Collins wrote to me suggesting that he and his wife should come out to Kenya and spend some time with me and the family and that he and I would create a book of our own. He said that he would publish, at their expense, whatever book I chose to do, knowing how badly let down I had been over the *Field Guide* books. He said he knew my artwork, and a book done between the two of us would not fail to be a success. I was *so* excited about this; at last, something good was about to happen in that field.

We made plans for Sir William and his wife's visit, and everything was ready for them. The last minute shopping done in Nanyuki, we collected the mail. To my utter horror, I received a telegram from the secretary to Sir William stating that Sir William Collins had suffered a sudden heart attack and passed away! This was a drastic blow, not only for his family, but to me. My world suddenly collapsed in huge disappointment: the book he and I planned together was not to be. I was devastated. I later spoke with one of his managers who came out to Nairobi, but there was no way in which they could now publish a book I might still try to do on my own. They said it had been entirely between Sir William Collins and me.

We had some visitors from Great Britain staying with us, amongst them, Robert Gillmor, the world's authority on herons. Gillmor, also a bird artist and photographer, took hundreds of photos of birds around the ranch and was very helpful with information about bird art, and I learned some useful tips. He told me about a World Wildlife Artists Exhibition that was to take place at the Mall Gallery in London and suggested I go over with my bird paintings to attend. I would have loved to have gone, but for various reasons, I was not able to go at the time the exhibition was to take place, so very kindly Robert Gillmor offered to take four of my bird paintings back with him. I later heard that all four paintings were voted in unanimously! I was thrilled. I was the only wildlife artist exhibiting who was not in attendance, which was sad—they had come from all over the world. The only paintings that were actually sold were those of Sir Peter Scott. The exhibition had been opened by Prince Bernhard of the Netherlands.

The well-known ornithologist and world authority on birds of prey, Dr. Leslie Brown, asked me to paint for the new books he was working on at the time: *Birds of Prey of Africa*. He was most insistent that I illustrate the entire five volumes. This would entail my signing a five-year contract to paint virtually nonstop, in order to complete the work in the given time. Leslie assured me that I would not be let down this time, knowing what had taken place with my previous experiences.

I wasn't at all sure that I could commit myself to such a tremendous project, and I explained this to him. He was adamant that I paint for his five volumes, telling me to give up my cattle trading business! "Susan," he said, "anyone can trade cattle, but not anyone can paint birds like you can. I insist you take up this contract. I will give you three months to give it serious thought. I am not in the best of health, and we need to complete this project within the five years."

I did think about it very seriously. He explained to me that at the end of it all, I would be a world-famous bird artist. I had asked what the income would be, and if I would acquire a decent income to live on at the end of five years hard work, to which he answered, "The money does not matter. You will be famous worldwide!"

Thinking about it, I couldn't see the point of being world famous if I didn't have any income to show for it. If I gave up my cattle business, and if not many people around the world bought bird paintings, where would that leave me? It all seemed too risky, and I didn't know whether I should take that risk or not. I had a very difficult time making my mind up. Nobody could do that for me.

I went back to see Leslie after three months, having rolled it over in my mind. I was concerned about the future and finally turned his offer down. Leslie was absolutely furious with me and thereafter refused to speak to me or my family ever again! As it turned out, it was the right decision for me, as, unfortunately, Leslie passed away from ill health two years later, so the volumes were hardly even started. If I had taken on the job, my paintings would have been to no avail.

Over a period of twenty or more years, I was commissioned to paint for Barclays Bank. They hung my work in several of their branches in Nairobi, including their Queensway branch, where we had accounts at the time, and their head offices. Barclays Bank printed a number of my paintings to send to their branches around the world, and I was paid royalties on each print. As a present, they gave, one of my finest eagle paintings to one of their top managers in London. I did extremely well from the Barclay commissions over all those years.

Fortunately I was able to sell my paintings to people all over the world during the 1980s and 90s. I would get commissions from people from various countries who were in Kenya on safari and send the pictures to them by DHL. It all worked out very well, and everyone was delighted with their pictures.

Friends I once knew used to go over to the USA to the hunter's convention meetings. One friend offered to take some of my paintings over to see if she could get sales for me. She took four of my finest bird paintings with her to show other people who would be at the meeting. I asked her to please bring them back if they were not sold by the time she was due to return to Kenya, and she agreed. While she was there, she happened to meet the owner of an art gallery who took great interest in the four bird paintings. He persuaded her to leave them with him, saying he could easily sell them from his gallery, and he would want me to send more. So, rather than lose out on potential sales, she left them with him. On her return, she gave me all the details of the gallery and the owner so that I could get in touch.

In due course, I wrote asking if the gallery had sold the paintings. I waited a considerable time, but there was no response. I wrote again and again, still no response whatsoever. I became very upset over the situation. This went on for a period of over four years; the gallery owner just would not reply to any of my letters. By now I was extremely worried. It seemed that my paintings must have been stolen by this gallery, so I had to accept the fact that I would never see the paintings again and would have to accept the loss.

My brother, Andrew, was taking out photographic safaris at the time and had a very nice man from America on safari. They spent part of the safari with us on Enasoit Ranch, and I happened to mention the incident to the young man, John by name, that it looked as though the artwork had been stolen. His immediate reply was "Don't you worry, Susan, I will get those paintings back for you, if you give me the details of the gallery."

Well, I couldn't believe that this could happen. I gave him all the details, however, and he and Andrew continued on their safari. I really didn't think that I would ever hear from John again. Shortly afterwards when I met up with Andrew, he informed me that his client, John, was in fact from the CIA.

Of course, I had not any idea of this while John was staying with us. Now, this put a new light on the situation and seemed likely that John would, indeed, get my paintings back. After he returned to the USA, we got his "Thank you" letter, for having looked after him in our home, and all he said about the matter of the paintings was that he would work on it and I *would* get them back. In the meantime, he sent me lovely photos of the Grand Canyon and we corresponded over other matters.

One day while doing the shopping, I received a very strange telegram in the post box. It read, "Please be at the New Stanley Hotel Foyer in Nairobi at"—whatever date—"and these will be there at the time stated."

I couldn't really make this out at all and didn't connect it with anything to do with the paintings. However, we flew in our aircraft to Nairobi on that particular day, and I went to the Stanley Hotel foyer at precisely the time stated. One of the lifts in the foyer opened, and there stood a man holding a large parcel. He stepped out looking around, and when saw me standing there, he briefly asked if I was Susan Hall. I replied that I was, whereupon he thrust the parcel into my arms and, without a single word, quickly disappeared back into the lift and the doors closed. I was left standing with the parcel, totally bewildered. On opening it, there were my four paintings, which had been lost for all those years! John, the CIA man, sent them back to me by private courier all the way from the USA.

One particular evening during the 1980s, we happened to be invited to a dinner party with Henry Roussel of Roussel Pharmaceuticals. We knew Henry and his family quite well, as they owned the ranch next to ours. We had a friend staying with us who had lived in Kenya for many years, but was currently living in England and had come out to see us. He suggested that I take some of my paintings over to show Henry, but I was rather shy and reserved over the matter. Our friend Kim, however, filled me with encouragement, so we loaded a few paintings of varying subjects into the Range Rover and drove out of our ranch through Ol Jogi, which belonged to the Roussels at that time, to his large and impressive house with its spectacular gardens and sweeping lawns, overlooking Africa and its wildlife.

The guests were celebrities from all parts of the world. The women were dressed in fine evening gowns from Paris and London, some with plunging necklines showing suntanned curves, and wearing the finest jewellery. The men, in tropical-style, open-neck shirts, which showed off their golden chests, and cream or light brown well-fitted slacks, stood in small groups or glided across the large veranda floor, everyone holding a crystal glass filled with some exotic drink. We were introduced to everyone, and some of the Frenchmen gave a slight bow taking my hand and gently touching it with their lips, and then flashing broad smiles.

The seating for dinner was arranged by name. Searching the tables, as there were several long tables set beautifully, I found mine and it so happened that I was seated next to Henry. Smartly dressed waiters served dinner on beautiful china plates, specially made to Henry's specifications, and wine in gold-rimmed wine glasses.

Henry had set my paintings out for all to view and had looked intently at all of them himself. As we were talking over dessert, he asked if he could buy the painting of the Spanish Lady. I explained that it was a present that I had given to my father, so, most unfortunately, I could not sell it to him. He was amazed, as nobody had ever refused to sell something to Henry Roussel. He said, "Susan, I really want that painting, and I am willing to pay whatever you ask."

"Sorry," I replied, "it belongs to my father."

"Then ask him if he will let you sell it to me. I will pay *anything.*"

"Well," I said, "it was a birthday present, so there is no way that it can be sold."

I had included it in the paintings I had taken over to give him an idea of my work. Henry was disappointed but then asked if I would paint a portrait of his wife and daughter, which he commissioned me to do, as well as several other subjects, one of which was a life-size macaw. Henry decided that the bird paintings I had shown him would be of great interest to Mr. Adnan Khashoggi, who would be coming with his entourage to have lunch with the Roussels the following Sunday. "Would you like to come and join them all and go swimming in the pool after lunch?" he asked me. He reminded me that swimsuits were not necessary. Nobody there bothered with them. I was somewhat shocked to think that I might be in the large, attractive pool with a lot of celebrities whom I had not met, minus my swimsuit. Henry said that I would be the only local person there, as everyone else would be his friends from overseas and, of course, Mr. Adnan Khashoggi and his entourage.

I thought about it while we enjoyed our after-dinner coffee; but decided that the scene and the company would not really be *me*, so I politely declined Henry's kind offer, but told him that I would love to visit him and his family again sometime soon. Henry very kindly offered to show my paintings to Adnan Khashoggi, so I left them with him. Around ten days later, I got a message from Henry via one of his managers to say that Mr. Khashoggi bought six of my bird paintings as presents for his children. I was delighted. Henri had all the cash for me and very kindly drove over to see me. He had my money tucked away in every pocket of his safari jacket and trousers. The next step was to count it all out. It was a very good sale and all credit to Henry's kindness in doing the deal for me.

Thereafter, Henry Roussel commissioned paintings from time to time. Much later, he introduced us to Alec Wildenstein, who happened to be staying with him, when we were invited to another of Henry's large luncheon parties.

After Adnan Khashoggi bought my bird paintings, he, of course, wanted to meet the artist. He obviously had heard about me from Henry and sent one of his bodyguards over to our ranch to ask if I would please go over to his ranch to join them for a lunch party. He was interested in looking at and purchasing more of my paintings. At the time, almost all of my artwork was with an agent at one of the Nairobi galleries, so I gave all the details to Mr. Khashoggi's bodyguard and asked if he would kindly pass on the information to Mr. Khashoggi. The bodyguard was very insistent that I still accept the invitation, but I politely declined.

A day or two later, a message for me from Mr. Khashoggi came with one of the ranch managers, a friend of ours actually. He was simply bringing the message, which was that Mr. Khashoggi refused to contact my agent and said he wanted me personally to go over to his hundred-thousand-acre ranch, Ol Pejeta, to have lunch and do an art deal, and I was to go alone.

I was now beginning to get rather concerned with the pressure that I was receiving. I was young and vulnerable, and most certainly would not have been able to hold my own in the company of the people I was being cajoled into joining. Friends of ours who knew a lot more about the situation and lifestyle of the company I would be involved with if I accepted these invitations, advised my parents to keep me at home for the time being. That "time being" lasted for two years. Finally, the pressure was off and I felt at ease again.

A few years later, Mr. Alec Wildenstein took over the Ol Jogi Ranch from Henry Roussel, so we came to know the entire family very well. I would often be asked to go over to give advice on some of the décor in the main house, such as where to hang a certain painting or where to place a preserved buffalo head, should it be hung above the fireplace or on one of the walls with plenty of space. I found it most interesting and enjoyed being asked my opinion to help with ideas for the main house.

At the time, Alec and his wife, Jocelyne, would often come over to our home for tea. They took great interest in my paintings. The first two paintings Alec bought from me were two bird of prey paintings. He wanted them for his son and daughter. Thereafter, he commissioned paintings from me every year, and for the next twenty-five years I was commissioned to paint some of their dogs, the marmoset monkeys, life-size macaws, and many other birds including various parrots and cockatoos, all in very great detail. Some of my paintings were kept to decorate the Ol-Jogi home, others taken to their homes in New York, Paris, London, and the Virgin Islands. It was a real challenge as the paintings were expected to be as perfect as the real subject: every feather on a bird, every vein in a leaf, rain drops on the leaves of a bush. I learnt to paint as a real perfectionist and enjoyed every moment of the challenge, and it all paid off extremely well.

We were invited to many dinner parties at the Wildenstein's' home on Ol Jogi, and I enjoyed the visits. It gave Mother and me a chance to really dress up. I used to make a new exotic evening gown for every occasion to which we were invited. On some of the occasions, it would be Diane's birthday, and every year I would give her one of my decorated eggs as a present when we were invited to the large dinner parties. The decorated eggs are also known as jewelled eggs. I use turkey eggs and cut little doors in the shell, line the inside of the shell with pretty coloured silks, paint the outer shell with various coloured vanishes, and decorate them with gold braid and jewels. To make stands for each egg is no easy task, but each one must have its own stand. The end result is a very unusual ornament. I was able to sell these to various shops in Nairobi at one time. They are rather a delicate ornament and need a protected place in which to stand. Each egg is an individual; no two are the same. The opening doors have tiny gold-chain fasteners. The rich, deep colour on the outer shell shows up dramatically when decorated with gold braids and beads of varying kinds.

I had spent a lot of time painting subjects in water colours for an exhibition in Nairobi. Some of my paintings were hanging in the Mashariki Art Gallery, which belonged to Mashariki Motors, or BMW. The gallery was in a prominent location in Nairobi City, and the manager of Mashariki at that time, Sean Garstin, was a friend. He was mainly in charge of selling beautiful BMW motor cars, and a young lady ran the gallery. She one day said to me, "Susan, why not ask Sean if you can have an exhibition here in the gallery?" So I did just that, and Sean very kindly offered to help me with the entire operation.

Not far down the street from the gallery was the shop where my paintings were being framed. It was December 1995, a good time of the year for an exhibition.

We made the dates for the show and had the paintings brought over from the framers. Sean hung all the paintings for me, a tremendous help, and we decorated the gallery with flowers and tables with white cloths ready for snacks for the opening night. We even situated one of the beautiful BMWs in the gallery with a bowl of flowers on its roof. The gallery looked perfect, the paintings hung to perfection.

Now we were thinking about the food and drinks for the opening evening, having sent out invitations to many embassies, banks, and a number of other prominent businesses. Sean, being an excellent cook and having a wonderfully large kitchen in his attractive home, said it would be no problem to organize all the snacks. We went off in one of the BMW cars to buy cheeses from the Brown's Cheese Factory, and then to one or two other places to get sparkling wines and soft drinks. Sean then made up the most delicious pâté to have with biscuits and various other tasties. He loaned me his best china plates and special glassware for the drinks. Everything looked fantastic.

We were all set for the opening. My parents were there, as were a number of special friends. The gallery looked spectacular, and people from the newspapers all showed up.

Disaster had taken place the evening before. One of the over-seas ambassadors was attacked by thugs and shot dead, which put a disastrous picture on people going out at night, particularly driving into the centre of the city. This had a dreadful, crushing effect on the opening of the exhibition. No embassy people were able to attend, and some of the prominent businessmen weren't able to attend either. The town was all but dead, and this hap-pened the very night before my opening. We had done so much work to make this exhibition a success and now …

The newspaper reporters did arrive. My parents were with me and friends from various parts of the country arrived, but the main guests who would have purchased the art were not able to attend.

Everything looked wonderful. The reporters took photos, which were in the papers the following day. Sean handed the drinks around to the guests who were able to attend, and people helped themselves to the delicious snacks that were all laid out beautifully. We had South American pipe music softly playing in the background.

It was a huge disappointment to us all that this disastrous incident had taken place, particularly the night before my open-ing. The exhibition continued for the following week, so people were in and out of the gallery to look at the art. There were a few sales and, in fact, enough to cover all costs, but nowhere near the sales that would have taken place had it not been for this unfortunate situation.

***

During 1996 and again in 2006, I visited my friends in the USA, both times to display some of my art. The first visit was to turn out as a most adventurous six weeks in some of America's most stunning countryside. All the states I travelled through were in the Southwest, and then there were parts of northern Mexico I was fortunate enough to visit. A great many parts that I explored reminded me very much of northern Kenya.

I started off my American travels in California, having landed in LA to stay with a friend who lived in a beautiful little "cowboy" town called Kernville. Another friend, Tom, took me flying in his Cessna 180 light aircraft over and around the Sierra Nevada Mountains, which was a stunning sight. We visited the magnificent forest of Sequoia trees (giant redwood trees) at a place called "Walk of 100 Giants."

I was invited on a white-water rafting trip with some friends of my friends, which turned out to be a huge and amazing experience for me, as I had never done it before. There were five of us in the inflatable dingy that was operated by a real expert. He was brilliant! We went over fast-rushing rapids and considerable sized waterfalls for around fourteen miles all on the Kern River. It was incredibly exhilarating, and I enjoyed the whole experience enormously.

After meeting a number of delightful people in California, I then flew with Tom in his Cessna to Tucson in Arizona to meet up and stay with my friend, Valerie. Valerie and I travelled all over the Southwest and parts of Mexico in her fabulous Buick Limousine. We spent my forty-eighth birthday in Nogalas on the Mexican-Arizona border. While having a delicious lunch, three dashing Mexican gentlemen came to sing and play their guitars to us!

We then spent several nights in a charming motel in Tombstone, Arizona, where I met more delightful cowboys and visited all the famous bars, including the Crystal Palace Bar, where I danced with the bouncer, Butch. He was the bouncer of all the Tombstone bars, and he gave me a large Tombstone silver coin as a keepsake. It is a most attractive Western town, full of history.

At The Big Steer Bar, in an area called Patagonia in South Arizona, we met a tall, handsome man who desperately wanted to prove himself to me by showing me his large, silver belt buckle won when he was riding a bull in a rodeo. We had drinks and danced with total strangers. It was all so friendly and happy, and I felt perfectly at ease in what was a completely strange place to me.

Valerie and I travelled to Texas Canyon and Cochise Stronghold in the Chiricahua Mountains in southeast Arizona. Having returned to Tucson for a few days to be with Valerie's husband, Bob, our next long "safari" was to Canyon De Chelly. Here, we hired a Jeep and driver and drove for many hours through the wonders of Canyon De Chelly, viewing the amazing sights of some of the Anasazi ruins, all built inside enormous caves and rock overhangs. The following day, the same Navajo guide, Lewis Yellowman, took me for a five-hour walk along the canyon floor. We visited some of his people who were living in very simple hogan dwellings, the women weaving beautiful rugs and the men just lazing about.

While on this most interesting walk, Lewis asked me if I would attend a special ceremony of the Navajo people. He said that no white man had ever been invited to such ceremonies, but that *I* would be a special guest. I was a little taken aback and most intrigued. I was unsure whether I should accept: I would be the only white person amongst hundreds of the Navajo Tribe, and I was in a strange country. I politely asked him if I could bring Valerie with me, and reluctantly he agreed, otherwise, I would have felt obliged to refuse.

Valerie and I went together in her car. The area was out in the open country, some distance from the canyon. There was a huge bonfire in the centre of a cleared area, surrounded by the Navajo's pickup trucks, all facing out with tail gates facing towards the fire, full of their food and drinks in plastic cool boxes. We were given camp chairs to sit on by Lewis Yellowman and looked after by him. The rest of the Navajo families ignored us in total. We most certainly felt quite out of place, as the only person who was friendly towards us was Lewis.

The men, almost all very overweight, who were dressed in blue jeans, check shirts, and Stetson hats, began to dance around the very large fire, chanting, as they would have done two hundred years ago. They were then joined by their overweight womenfolk. Now there was a crescendo of amazing chanting going on. Closing one's eyes, one could imagine the scene as it would have been several hundred years before.

It was all very enchanting with the stars shining down from a dark, clear sky. Lewis, who warned us that in no uncertain

Susan M. Hall

terms were we to join any of the dancing, even if we were asked, had the gall to come to me and ask me to dance with him. I flatly refused, but later he came up and asked again. Valerie and I looked at one another and decided that the time had come for us to gracefully depart. Lewis was most upset that we were leaving, but it was time to move out of this most amazing experience.

I had not wanted to camp in a designated campsite, and we were very fortunate that Lewis's father-in-law agreed to let us camp in his area, again, something not normally offered to white people. Lewis's father-in-law, Johnson, gave me the option of staying in the Navajo Reservation for a period of up to ten years if I wanted to. Again, this was a most generous offer—they did not offer white people such a facility—so I was extremely honoured.

Later, when we were telling other Americans about my experiences with the Navajo people, they were completely dumbfounded and told me how greatly honoured I was, first to be invited to one of their ceremonies, and second to be allowed to camp in their territory, and finally to be invited to remain on the reservation for the following ten years. The Navajo were intrigued that I came from Africa. It was an amazing incident that I shall forever remember. I was indeed, highly honoured by the Navajo.

From there we went to Monument Valley, then into Utah, and on into Colorado. The Rocky Mountains were short of snow. Unfortunately, there was a snow drought, so the snow we were seeing was from the previous year. We stayed with a friend of Valerie's named Joey. She lived in a lovely location with a stream running through her garden. We visited a charming town called Telluride, which is at a nine-thousand-foot elevation above sea level and set close to the mountains.

From Colorado, Valerie and I headed to New Mexico and visited Taos and some of the Pueblo Indian homesteads. We went to some fantastic art galleries where some of the artwork was stunning and amongst the best I had ever seen. I loved the style of the Pueblo buildings.

Back into Arizona and to the South Rim of the Grand Canyon, we met up with Dr. Chuck, a good friend of Valerie and Bob's. He very kindly offered to take me climbing down into and back up the Grand Canyon. We camped close to the rim, but not in view of the canyon, as there was a lot of bush between our campsite and the canyon. It was desperately hot down in the Grand Canyon. Chuck and I had left Valerie in camp and ventured off for the whole day witnessing breath-taking views all around and down to the Colorado River seven or eight thousand feet below. The climb down and back up was hard going, mainly due to the breathless heat and my previously damaged knee. The rim of the canyon in the area where we were located was around eight thousand feet above sea level, so it was very cool in our tents at night.

It was nearing the time for me to leave the wonderful time I had spent with my friend, Valerie, to meet up with my friends from California again, so we drove to Zion National Park in Utah to a small hotel and met up with them. The following day, it was a very sad good-bye for Valerie and me.

My amazing trip now continued with Kat and Jess. We walked The Narrows, the narrowest section of Zion Canyon. One walks along the river with the canyon walls going straight up a thousand feet out of the river towards the sky. We walked up the mountain sides to a place called Angel's Landing, which commanded outstanding views.

Our next adventure was to Bryce Canyon, another amazing scene where we did a lot of walking. Being summer, the weather was much like I was used to in Northern Kenya. From Bryce, we went to stay in a lodge on the Northern Rim of the Grand Canyon, where we had our evening meal looking out of enormous plate glass windows, almost on the very edge of the canyon—an unforgettable experience.

Mike, a friend of Tom's, met up with Kat and me to take a walk down Hurricane Wash in the Escalante area. We walked for three days with backpacks and covered around thirty miles round trip. We bathed at the bottom of a beautiful waterfall and drank clear water from the Escalante River. Mike took us to

215

Moon House, a remote area where there are ancient Anasazi ruins, fascinating ruins built under a huge overhang of rocks, all made from mud bricks.

Continuing our journey, we drove for most of that day to Valley of the Gods, still in Utah. We slept the night out under the stars next to enormous clay castles or buttes. The following day we drove through part of the Nevada Desert and then on to the well-known Monument Valley.

Having been camping and driving through the desert areas, I was not prepared for the surprise that Mike arranged for me. It was dark and, as we came over the brow of a hill, there in front was a sea of lights shinning ahead of us. I asked where on earth they were taking me, and it turned out to be Las Vegas! I was initially quite horrified. What a drastic shock it was to me. We found a hotel for the night on the outskirts of town, got ourselves all dressed up, and went out to explore Vegas. We had dinner in the Excalibur Casino, and then moved on to the Luxor Casino, it was all rather out of my sphere.

Mike continuously fed me tequila, a wonderful drink. I soon relaxed, and we had a marvellous time exploring the casinos of Vegas. We finally got to bed at three in the morning.

Next morning we journeyed into Death Valley, an area which is two hundred and eighty two feet *below* sea level. It is hot there in summer, but not quite as hot as Kenya's Chalbi Desert.

After staying for a few days in Tom's house in Inyokern, California, Mike and I took off to climb the Sierra Nevada Mountains. We camped on the desert below, north of Bishop, and the following morning, climbed up to around eleven thousand feet and right into the snow area. I never experienced snow, so it was amazing for me. Walking past several beautiful lakes and through forested areas and across streams before reaching the snow line was perfectly delightful. I even made snowballs and threw them at Mike! It was all such fun, and so different from what I was used to. In all, it was an up and down eighteen-mile walk. When we got back down to the bottom, Mike suggested taking me out to dinner, as we hadn't yet set up our camp, so we changed in the pine forest and enjoyed a nice dinner with wine. Later, Mike and I camped back on the desert area. We found some hot springs and sat with our toes in the warm pool, chatting and enjoying more wine. Mike and I drove back to Tom's place, and then the sixty miles to Kat's home the following day.

Now it was the end of this most amazing holiday, and it was sad saying good-bye to Mike.

I had met an interesting man by the name of George, who wanted me to go back to California with all my artwork. He was willing to take me all over the USA and had said that it would be no trouble at all to sell my art. He was willing to pay for the entire project, including all my flights back and forth from Kenya. He said he would get everything he invested back when he sold my art. It sounded a wonderful idea. When I came to leave, George hired a beautiful Chrysler convertible to take me to Los Angeles airport. He said that if we went into the art project together, I would very soon become a wealthy woman and own my own Chrysler within two years.

As things turned out, the project never even got off the ground. My fault entirely, as I had already met an Englishman who was later to become my husband, so I felt it only right to remain at home and not go off around America with George for several months at a time.

During July and August of 2006, while my husband was in England to see family and for medical reasons, I went to USA again. I stayed with Kat and her husband and then Valerie once more. We made some lovely trips together. San Francisco was a delightful city, and the drive there was most interesting. Later, Valerie and I travelled considerably, the same as we did during my 1996 visit, and we went to Mexico again.

The last, most fascinating time was a day in Disneyland, California, the day before leaving the USA to go back home to Kenya via the UK. This was the last time that I ever saw my best friend Valerie, as some years later she sadly passed away from lymphoma.

***

I had flown down to Cape Town several times in the hopes of creating some art business. While there, I travelled around the cape with Nigel and through the Garden Route. We went up Table Mountain, and then a few days later we went to visit a number of vineyards to test the wines. I very much enjoyed the short times I spent in the cape.

Again, my last trip to Cape Town to visit Nigel in 2006 was the last time I ever saw our special friend. He passed away from cancer the same year as my wonderful friend, Valerie.

Telephone 01-493 5321
Telegrams: Herakles London, S.W.1
Telex: Herakles London 25611

Chairman
Sir William Collins, C.B.E.

Collins · Publishers

14 ST JAMES'S PLACE, LONDON, S.W.1

AIR MAIL   26th August, 1976

Dear Susan,

At last I think we have managed to get our plans
fixed. I am arriving in Nairobi on the morning of Friday,
8th October. I am probably spending the weekend with Joy
Adamson and flying on to Bukabu on the 11th, and will be
there until the 15th. My wife is flying out to Nairobi
on the 13th, and we wondered whether it would be suitable
if we came up to you for say a long weekend from the
Saturday to the Tuesday (16th to 19th).

A very nice man, Nigel Guild, who looks after our
interests in Nairobi said he would try and get in touch with
you, but he tells me today that you are not on the telephone.
He is trying to get an earlier message to you about our plans.

I told him that I imagined we would motor up, but he
says there is an air strip and we might possibly fly. If
these dates don't suit you and your parents perhaps you could
send a message to him at his office.

His address is:

J.L. Morison Son & Jones (Kenya) Ltd.
Bandəri Road,
P.O. Box 40196,   Tel. No. 556999
Nairobi

Perhaps if you go to Nanuki you could telephone him from there.

I have still not had a reply to my last letter to
John Williams.   Yours ever,
Miss Susan Hall,
Enasoit Ranch,
P.O. Box 29,
Nanyuki,
Kenya, East Africa

219

Susan M. Hall

From: Sir Peter Scott CBE DSC

THE NEW GROUNDS
SLIMBRIDGE
GLOUCESTER GL2 7BT

Tels: Cambridge (045-389) 333
Cables: Wildfowl Dursley

Dear Miss Hall
    John Williams has shown me some Transparencies
of the lovely plates you have done for the new
Field Guide and I write to congratulate you on them.
    I believe long, long ago that you came to a lecture
of mine in Nakuru, & I like to hope that that
was one of the factors which led to your interest
in natural history — which I have found such a
wonderful recipe for an enjoyable life.
    I hope we'll meet again one day, meanwhile I am

waiting impatiently for the new Field Guide with some
of your plates in it, & for the wild flower book John
has told me about.
    All best wishes -
        Yours sincerely
            Peter Scott.

P.S. Keep painting — it's important.

220

THE DESIGNING AND
BUILDING OF SAMSARA

It looks into the game park
Where Sable and Elephants roam
And all around grow the African flowers,
Where the Honey bees drone.
                                   —Thelma G. Hall

A soft glow from the evening sun cast a pale-pink hue on the
Moorish archways of Samsara. The lime-wash building, a
small Arab-style house that I call my baby palace, is situated
on a steep hillside along the Southern Shimba Hills overlooking a beautiful forested valley within a game reserve. The name
Samsara is a Sanskrit word meaning "endless birth, death, and
rebirth; a never ending circle, peace, harmony and the never
ending love of natural things and pure freedom."

My brother, Andrew, and I bought land close to one another
with the long-term view of spending our old age side by side,
but sadly and most unfortunately, this was not to be, due to his
passing away the same year I purchased the land.

My land is approximately twelve miles inland from the
Indian Ocean and thirty miles south of Mombasa. The drive to
Samsara through the little African farms studded with coconut
palms is delightful. Huge mango trees create cool shade in
which the women, dressed in coloured *gitengi* materials, sit
with their small children playing around them. Their earth-floor
houses are made from coral and mud, thatched with coconut
fronds made into mats, which form a very cool roofing mate-

rial. Coconut palms, their fronds waving in the coastal breezes, banana plants and cassava, all grow around the homesteads.

I designed and built Samara in the 1990s on thirty-five acres of very attractive country. I bought it in March 1991. Samsara's interior is also painted in lime wash with small arched niches in the walls adorned with deep-blue glass ornaments. A round, antique, carved table from Zanzibar graces one end of the sitting room and is surrounded by coloured rugs. The antique dining room chairs, with woven string seats and wooden backs and arms with cream cushions, bordered with silk burnt orange design, stand out against the white walls. Two large chairs, woven from papyrus reeds, sit snuggly in the rounded corners of the opposite end, with nests of scatter cushions, some in white with exotic gold braid trimmings, others covered with rich red and gold material from India. A Lamu-style, carved baby's bed rests against one wall, adorned with richly coloured scatter cushions. An old antique gramophone, "His Master's Voice," has its place in the sitting room.

My bedroom is very sparsely furnished. The bed is an ornate carved Lamu-style bed covered in a gorgeous Indonesian bed cover. A chair, a simple chest of drawers, and rugs covering part of the mazeras stone floor, are all that are needed.

Samsara is my haven of peace, the place I go to be away from everything and everyone except a few very close friends who come to visit and spend a night or two enjoying the views and watching the elephants wander across the hills and around the forest. Elephants frequently come into my garden at night, as do water buck and occasional sable antelope. There are no glass windows in Samsara, just wooden shutters and black, twisted iron bars. The breeze blows right through from one side of the house to the other through the wide, open shutters.

The rolling hillsides are heavily covered in grass and hundreds of short doum palms. The palms around my little lime-washed homestead have grown considerably, having been protected from the dreadful bush fires that the local neighbours light each year in order to burn the coarse grass, ready for the rainy season when fresh new green grass shoots up with the first shower. The fires get totally out of hand, and sweep across the land with a great wind behind, burning everything in their path, including small animals and huge forest trees.

Sitting in the evenings outside on the coral chip patio, which is right on the edge of the extremely steep hillside, one looks down into the wonderful forested valley, most of which is in the game reserve, but a little of it is on my land. It gives me such pleasure to be part of this enchanting scene. The sunsets are exquisite: golden clouds streak the sky, turning to red, yellow, and even a deep purple as we sit sipping our drinks, the humidity high, after hot days.

The valleys of the Shimba Hills are unique with streams flowing off the higher areas, joining up to form a clear babbling river surrounded by enormous, tall forest trees, all in varying colours of greens. Waterfalls here and there flowing over rocks are canopied by these huge and magnificent trees. The river flows in the valley below my house, but it is not visible from the house as it winds its way through the forest. We can hear it, however, even at the driest time of the year. From my veranda, I can see the Usambara Mountains on a clear day way to the south in Tanzania. While building Samsara, I would frequently drive the five-hundred-mile distance from our ranch, Enasoit, all the way to Samsara alone. It was indeed a very lonely trip, but I would always spend one night with friends in Nairobi, and then the second and third nights with friends along the way. I would always be extremely relieved to arrive at my destination.

To keep myself alert on these long journeys, I would listen to some of my favourite music, including the South American panpipe music. I would even sing! It was an enormous relief when I completed building Samsara, which took several years of hard work. My parents and I could then enjoy the peace and tranquillity of Samsara.

Part Six
Romance

FRIENDS OF THE PAST

Those were sad times, when without you
I watched worlds and days come up,
And then again go down.

　　　　　　　　　—Japanese wisdom

When I was sixteen, a good friend of ours, who had known
us since I was around six years old, wanted to marry me.
He was eleven years my senior.

I was, of course, very fond of Patrick. He spent an awful lot
of time with us and almost became part of the family. The problem was that the business he was in unfortunately failed. He felt
that he didn't have the backing to be able to support me, and so
he was very reluctant to ask my father for my hand in marriage.
I felt that I was too young anyway, and, although I was very
close to him, I thought of him more as a brother. Later I began
to feel differently, but by that time he was ready to leave the
country, so we didn't see him again for many years.

We did, however, exchange Christmas cards, and he and my
mother kept in touch from time to time by letter. It was around
twenty-four years later when Patrick was on his way to England
that he stopped off in Kenya to see us. It was a fantastic reunion,
as nothing had changed. My parents, Patrick, and I got along
as though we had never been apart. We talked and laughed and
everything was just the same, and the gap of all those years
apart was closed in minutes.

He was, of course, married with children by this time. However, before leaving he told me that he was still very much in
love with me and always would be. I was very sad and upset to

227

see him leave again. We spent five wonderful days, the four of us together.

Patrick and I kept in touch by letter on occasion and met up every few years thereafter. It was terribly upsetting and sad when he became sick, and I learned of his passing. It happened the same year that I lost my other best friend, Valerie. Losing two of my closest friends in one year was more than I could bear. Patrick was a lifelong friend, and I miss him awfully.

During 1967 and 1968, I was very friendly with one of the game wardens who worked out of Maralal and Samburu Districts as well as Laikipia. Hugh was a handsome, dark-haired man whom I had met at the Aero Club of East Africa in Nairobi. We became good friends, as he was working in our area and would fly in to see me quite often while doing his wildlife rounds in the wildlife department Piper Cub. Hugh used to fly over the house and sometimes drop notes out of the aircraft window, hoping I would get them! Sometimes the notes would end up in the top of an Acacia tree so I couldn't reach them. Other times I would find notes in the bush months later, asking me to meet up for a dinner date in Nairobi. He must have wondered why I never turned up!

Our friendship continued for a number of years until Hugh was transferred to another district in the country.

***

At age twenty-four, I became friendly with a blond-haired man who was a geologist prospecting in our area. We often went out for the day, sometimes to the Mount Kenya Safari Club on the slopes of Mount Kenya for a nice, relaxing lunch. We would wander around the grounds, taking photos and generally enjoying the peace and surrounds. Other times I would go fishing with Andy, not that I was interested in fishing, but he enjoyed it. We would take a picnic and some wine and relax on the river bank. Andy came all the way out to the ranch often to take me out. He was a short man, a little stocky with thick, blond hair.

We had a good report and would often sing together while travelling along the rough, dusty roads.

Andy asked me to go and live with him in Malaysia, but my life was in Africa, and I couldn't think of leaving.

At the same time as my friendship with Andy, I also became friendly with a very tall, handsome British army captain, who came out to Kenya from time to time with the army. We became good friends, and the relationship lasted for a number of years. I even visited Philip's home in the UK.

While he was based in Kenya, we met up often and went out for the day and had dinners when we met in Nairobi. I became very fond of Philip and was thoroughly miserable when he was finally transferred back to the UK for good.

I was feeling so despondent that I decided to go on a holiday to the UK with my grandmother, who was going to stay a while with her brother in Nottingham. There was no point in looking up Philip, as I knew full well that his life would never bring him back to Africa.

Later on during our time in England, about a week before leaving to come home to Kenya, I met the son of my great uncle's bank manager. He wanted to know all about Kenya, as he was planning to book a safari. Jo came round to the house during the morning, and I explained as much as I could about what he could expect and what wildlife he would no doubt see on a safari in Kenya. Jo asked me if I would like to go round to his parents' house for dinner that evening. I was reluctant at first, but was encouraged by my uncle to go, so Jo came to pick me up at about six in the evening. He was an estate agent, and we chatted all the way to his parents' home.

Dinner was very English. I was shy, and it took me ages to struggle through what was actually a delicious meal. The evening was very pleasant though, and I enjoyed their company. Afterwards, Jo took me to a nearby pub to meet some of his friends and to enjoy a drink. When we arrived back at my uncle's home, Jo asked me if I would join him out to dinner the following evening. It seemed a nice idea, so I accepted.

We enjoyed another evening together, and on the way back to the house he parked the car in a farm gateway, took me into his arms, and, to my utter astonishment and shock, asked me to marry him—after only two evenings out together! Of course, I replied with a firm *no*, as I pointed out that we didn't know one another at all.

The following day we went out for a drink of delicious cider and a snack lunch. I was leaving for London the day after, and he was determined that one day we would marry! As we said our good-byes, we arranged that he would come and stay at the ranch with me when he came out for the safari.

I left for London with my grandmother, and, unbeknown to me, Jo had driven all the way from Nottingham to London hoping to catch me at the airport before we left. But he had been caught in a traffic jam, so missed me. I only knew this after I got back to Kenya and received my first letter in the mail from him.

Jo was medium height, fairly slim with light brown hair, and a very happy face. We were reacquainted in Nairobi a few months later after he had done several weeks' safari around Kenya. He came back home to the ranch for another two weeks. During that time, I took him to a number of places of interest: we took picnics out into the wilderness, and I showed him all our cattle and the ways in which we ran the ranch. The time together was enjoyable and started to become rather romantic. Time and time again he asked me to marry him, but I could not bring myself to make that commitment. He left Kenya telling me that he would apply for a job out here, so as to be near me.

We wrote letters to one another very often. I was always eager to check our mailbox every time we went to Nanyuki shopping. After around six months, he wrote to say that he had secured a job with an estate agent company in Nairobi. I couldn't believe it! He had done just what he set out to do.

After securing a house to live in around the Muthaiga area, Jo visited me on the ranch every weekend. Every week he asked me to marry him. The romance went on for over two years.

I was on safari in the north of Kenya with my parents. My longing for the wilderness, the beauty of the vast mountain ranges and the deserts, and this amazing life I had always known, all made my mind up for me. I would never be able to leave this wild type of lifestyle, and I knew full well that Jo would one day return to live in England. I just could not bring myself to marry Jo.

After I returned from safari, I went down to Nairobi to do various jobs and up to Jo's office where we made arrangements to have lunch together.

I told him once and for all that there was no way in which we could be married, due to the fact that his life would take him back to Britain one day, and that my life was here ... in Africa. I said to Jo that I would always be his trusted friend, but could never marry him. He finally accepted the situation and our romance slowly dwindled.

When I eventually had my weekends to myself, I felt an enormous weight lifted off my shoulders—at last I felt free again! Without realizing it fully, I felt myself slowly being channelled into a lifestyle I knew I could never accept. Although I enjoyed our romance during those years, I felt that I was being trapped, and now I was free once again.

I did not want to get so involved again for a very long time, but was very content to enjoy friendships, without deep involvement.

I had my cattle business to run, and a successful art business. I was totally enthralled with the exploratory safaris we were doing in Northern Kenya. I wanted nothing to change the wonders of the wilderness that I was so involved in.

After Andrew passed away, I felt totally devastated, and there seemed to be no happiness left.

We had known Clive, a very successful cattle rancher, for many years and, indeed, since I was fourteen years old. He also was suffering from a traumatic experience at the time, so each time we met up, we seemed to make one another happier. He was about twelve years older than I was. Both of us were involved with cattle business and ranching, so had a lot in common. My parents and I would go over to visit and be shown his remarkable Boran cattle. We very much enjoyed these visit, and he and I got along very well.

Clive and I decided to start going out and continued in this way for over a year. He would come over to Enasoit, and we would go to his ranch at Kifuku. He and I travelled to many places around Kenya, which was most enjoyable, and I met some lovely friends of his. Our friendship helped us both accept and get through the traumatic times that we were suffering in our own way.

After that first year, I started to spend time with Clive on Kifuku. We lived in a small cottage on the edge of the most fantastic, manmade reservoir, around sixty or more acres of water, which would fill from the flow during the rainy season from small seasonal streams coming off the land around. This was all created and built by Clive, probably the largest area of water created by just one man. It was a magnificent creation.

I would spend several weeks at a time on Kifuku, and then come home to visit my mother and father for a while. Our relationship became quite romantic over the following year, and Clive decided that we should build a house of larger dimensions than the cottage we were living in, also beside the dam. So, together we designed it and started to build in Basalt Rock off the ranch, of which there was abundance. The walls were three feet thick and all done in dry stone walling. A lot of my influence went into it, particularly all the Moorish archways that we created. The rounded corners and many other features were my ideas as well. The house was almost complete, Clive had done a lot of the hand work, and the metal and wood work was all done with his fair hands. Some of the heavy wooden doors were arched. It all looked unique.

We were still working on the house when I began to wonder whether I was doing the right thing to go home, and then give up everything to move all my belongings over to Kifuku. I began to miss my life on Enasoit, and my studio where I worked for many years creating art of many kinds. I was now beginning to feel that perhaps my life with Clive on a permanent basis may not be quite what we both expected. Clive was beginning to feel the same. We had helped each other through very difficult times, and we both appreciated that very much, but now we wondered whether it was entirely right for us to remain together.

We decided to split up. It was a very sad time, and we were just not sure what we wanted from one another. We did, however, remain very close friends indefinitely.

After I returned home to Enasoit to continue my life where I had left off, I met up with a very good primary school friend, Roger, whom I had known since I was about nine years old; he would have been about ten. We had been friends in our late teens as well.

He used to fly in to Enasoit with my cousin David to see me. We were both extremely shy, so never really got to going out together. Having gone our separate ways, we didn't see one another for many years. When we ran into each other after all those years at my cousin's house in Nairobi, we decided to go out to dinner at the Norfolk Hotel. It was amazing how after so long we rekindled our friendship. We were both single again and decided that our friendship could blossom.

Roger and I started to meet up whenever possible and when he could get time off work. He would come to Enasoit, and we would go back to Nakuru together where he lives, and then spend time at Naivasha. We made several trips to the coast together and found that we got along extremely well. We stayed at my Shimba Hills property a few times. Our relationship was a sincere and close friendship, as it always had been.

Roger, a good looking man of average height, always has a lovely warm smile. That smile will remain in my thoughts, always. We were not madly in love, but had this wonderful report. We made a promise to one another that if either of us fell in love for real with someone else, we would immediately tell the other. I did not think for one moment that it would be me. But …

Roger and I have remained indefinite friends, although we don't see one another very often now.

THE LOVE OF MY LIFE

A vehicle arrived with friends from England who had been on a picnic with family.

I was busy in my studio at our big ranch house, when mother called me to say they arrived for tea, so I left my work and went down to the sitting room. They were seated near the large picture windows as I walked into the spacious lounge. A heavily built man was sitting on one of the wide window ledges, so I went up and introduced myself.

I was wearing shorts—it had been a hot day—and as I had been brought up in the luxury of the tropical sunshine and had a healthy outdoor ranching lifestyle, I was slim and strong from the energetic life.

I noticed how he looked at me. He was handsome with a shock of thick, white hair. We sat talking for a while, and then I offered to go on a game drive with them around the ranch.

I sat in the back of the Toyota with Keith and pointed out the various animals. We talked a lot. I was very aware of Keith's presence and his arm stretched out along the back of the seat behind my neck. We had seen a heavily pregnant cheetah strolling through the thick acacia bush. I kept my head turned away towards the window, trying to avoid looking at Keith, and gazing out at the scenery, yet not really seeing but feeling the nearness of this big, gentle-looking man.

After we returned to the house, mother invited them all to come for lunch in a few days' time. I really looked forward to this, and so, it seemed, did Keith

They duly arrived, and I handed round drinks. After they quenched their thirst with cool beers taken from the old kerosene refrigerator, I ushered them into the large dining room and showed everyone to their places around the table. Mother brought in a dish of steaming beef casserole, saffron rice, and green peas, while father poured white wine into silver goblets. I handed plates of a floral design to the three guests, who helped themselves to lunch from the wooden trolley. I couldn't help noticing how tall Keith was as he stood waiting to serve the food onto his plate. His thick, creamy-white hair had a slight wave that caressed his forehead. He had a suntanned face from the days he had been staying in Kenya. He was dressed in a pair of well-cut grey shorts and a light-beige short-sleeved shirt, which fitted his broad shoulders snuggly. He looked younger than his fifty-seven years, his smile warm and gentle.

The clinking of knives and forks against plates seemed loud, as everyone enjoyed their lunch. Keith looked up from his plate across at me—I was opposite him—his soft grey-green eyes looking directly into my large brown ones fringed with lashes lightly brushed with mascara.

He noticed my rich, fair hair, streaked golden from years in the hot African sun. I wore it up in a twist at the back of my head, held secure by two carved wooden sticks. As our eyes met, I smiled shyly at him and our eyes were locked for what seemed an age. My heart leaped as I felt the blood rush to my tanned face. I could hardly manage to finish my meal, the excitement within me was overpowering. After the dessert of caramel custard and cream, everyone moved back into the spacious sitting room with its plush Persian rugs and Arab chests. As I walked through to the kitchen to pour the coffee, Keith joined me and, while I was pouring, he talked to me about solar lighting as a possibility for lighting for my newly built house on the Shimba Hills. I was listening intently, but my mind was in a complete whirl! Keith followed me into the kitchen just to be near me. He was burning inside with immeasurable power to take me into his arms and hold me close forever, but instead he kept his hands clasped firmly behind his back. I trembled as I handed him a cup of strong, hot coffee. He took it from me and stood looking at me, not knowing quite what to say next.

We started slowly back towards the sitting room. As we reached the door, we were standing so close, I looked up at him, and he bent his head and lightly kissed the top of my nose. I looked at Keith wide-eyed with surprise, and then lifted my head higher so that his lips brushed mine ever so tenderly, and then we walked silently to join the others in the sitting room. I sat looking out through the large picture windows in the room as the conversations took place, which now became meaningless to me. I glanced at Keith, who was sitting in a relaxed position, his shoulders slightly drooped, and looking down with a faint frown on his face, deep in thought.

Later, I said that I would be going to Nanyuki on the following Sunday to a hospital fate, so we arranged to meet there on that day. Keith's eyes lit up with a sparkle at the chance of seeing me again and hastily said that he would much look forward to Sunday. He would definitely be there, so we would meet again. We were already dominating one another's thoughts.

I found myself willing the next four days away; nothing else seemed relevant any more. Keith was on my mind continuously.

On the Saturday, I washed and set my hair. I chose a long Indian skirt and white frilled blouse to wear, with a wide belt for trim, and placed them ready on my bedroom chair. The following morning after I completed a hasty breakfast, I brushed out my long hair and piled it high on the crown of my head, brushing each lock to form golden curls. After a last look in the long mirror, I left the house and drove to Nanyuki in my Suzuki pickup. On arrival at the fate, I put on a fresh coat of pale brown lipstick and a puff of powder on my nose, glanced at my reflection in the rear view mirror, and then headed for the area where the fate was taking place.

The first person to appear to greet me was Keith. We both had big smiles for each other. They were serving soft drinks at the fate, so we both enjoyed a passion fruit juice with soda water. While wandering around, Keith gently took my hand in his. He said, "Susan, what is it? What is happening to us?"

I simply replied, "I don't honestly know what it is, but something has happened to us."

Wandering around, we looked at all the small items on sale, all the while talking with each other, totally oblivious of the stares from my friends and acquaintances and neighbours who were all so used to seeing me alone or with my parents.

Later, we came upon the drinks stall again. Keith asked me what I would like, and I replied that I would love a glass of red wine, so Keith returned from the stall with two glasses of rich red wine, which we sipped as we chatted with one another, completely engrossed and enchanted with each other and unaware of what was taking place around us. Later we helped ourselves to a salad lunch and sat on the green grass lawn together, a little distance away from the main crowd.

It was now time for me to think about returning home, so I asked Keith if I could drive him back to his sister's house in town. We climbed into my tiny Suzuki, the seats being close together. We were unable to contain ourselves a moment longer and fell simultaneously into each other's arms. His tender lips covered mine in a hot, passionate kiss, and my heart was beating with immeasurable emotion. There was no doubt in our minds that we were falling passionately in love.

It seemed a hopeless situation: Keith lived in the middle of England, and I in the heart of the African wilderness. All we wanted was to be together. It was a wild and impossible dream.

Romance

Out of the shadows came a light,
With smiling eyes, and words of love,
With gentle—and romantic touch.
                                    —Susan M. Hall

K eith and I knew that we would be heartbroken when he left to return to the U.K. We exchanged addresses and made a promise to keep in touch by letter as often as possible. We would not lose contact with each other, no matter what.

On saying our last good-bye, Keith took me in his arms. The hot tears burned my cheeks. He kissed me, gently at first, and then his lips were hard on mine, and he pulled my body close to his. For the first time he told me that he loved me, and I told him that I felt the same. My heart was burning with feelings for him and the sadness of parting. All we could look forward to was letters and occasional phone calls, as and when I would be near a telephone.

A few days later I happened to be in Nairobi staying with a friend. I mentioned this to Keith and gave him the phone number, so we were able to talk over the phone for about fifteen minutes. I planned a trip to the USA. The flight was via Amsterdam, so we arranged over the phone to meet at the airport. I would have a three-hour wait for the connecting aircraft. We now much looked forward to the confirmed date that we would see each other again, even if only for three hours.

The days that followed rolled by very slowly; time seemed to stand still. I wrote something to Keith every day and posted the letter when I eventually went to the post office, which was around once a week.

The day finally arrived for me to fly to the USA via Amsterdam. My parents and I were staying in Nairobi, and the night before leaving I got a call from Keith. It was wonderful to hear his voice and confirmation that he would be there at the airport in Amsterdam to meet me when I arrived. My heart was pounding, I was so excited.

It was a night flight, but I simply could not sleep a wink. On arrival at six in the morning Amsterdam time, all the passengers left the plane to walk along a tube-like passage towards the "Arrivals" area. My heart was in my mouth, and I was quite terrified at being out in the big wild world and so far from home. I was simply not used to it. My heart missed several beats as I saw, at the end of the tube, a man standing there with creamy white hair wearing a red pullover. There he was!

We were in each other's arms after what seemed to us like a thousand years, and now nothing else mattered. Keith and I spent three very short hours together in a small airport hotel room. We held each other so tightly and did not want to let go. We talked a lot and decided once again that we could not exist without one another. There were problems and huge hurdles to overcome on his side, but we simply decided that we would keep meeting up, one way or another, with the intention of one day being together, but at this stage it was a long, distant dream, a dream we hoped would come true one day.

Before boarding the plane for Los Angeles, we made an arrangement to meet again on my return journey in around six weeks' time. It would be an eleven-hour stopover, so much more time to be together. Another very sad good-bye with hugs, kisses and tears, as we parted. I was on my way.

While I was in America, I received faxes from Keith—some positive, some negative, due to the difficulties of his circumstances. This upset me drastically, as it seemed at the time that our dreams were being shattered. To try and think of a future without Keith was unthinkable, as I knew deep down that I could never forget him.

Several weeks later when it was almost time for me to leave America, I had another fax from Keith. He had managed to sort out some of his major problems and confirmed that he would be there at Amsterdam Airport to meet me again; he confirmed this with a phone call. I was so relieved. It gave me an enormous lift, and I now looked forward with all my heart and being to seeing him again.

The long flight was exhausting. I arrived at 11.40 am Amsterdam time. There were people milling around at the end of the long passage, but amongst them I saw to my great delight and relief the tall, familiar figure standing looking round. He caught site of me just before I reached him. The overwhelming joy when we met was apparent, as we clung to each other with wide, happy smiles. We could hardly believe that we were in each other's arms again. Keith booked a room in the Mercury Hotel at the airport for us to spend the eleven hours together in private. We talked a lot during those hours about our future and how we might possibly be able to spend time together, and one day we could plan to be together forever.

We made plans for Keith to come and visit me in Kenya in a couple of months' time. This was a wonderful plan that would keep us living in hopes and anticipation. Before getting ready to leave, Keith gave me a lovely gift: a gold heart-shaped locket and chain, a treasure which I wore often from then on.

It was heart wrenching having to part again, and we held each other close and talked of our coming reunion. My huge tears fell on Keith's shirt, wetting it down the front; he was close to tears himself. With our final kiss good-bye, his lips tightly over mine, he could taste the salt from my fallen tears. I looked at him with blurred vision and then turned to walk onto the plane.

For the following two months, we lived for one another's letters and counted the slow days, waiting to meet up again.

As he came through customs pushing his trolley with his luggage, Keith looked at the sea of faces waiting for arriving friends and wondering where I was. I was right there and got hold of his arm as I realised he hadn't spotted me. He was very relieved to see me, and I to see him! This was a very joyful time for us. This time we were to spend six weeks together.

As we drove away from the airport in my old Range Rover, we beamed at each other with sheer joy and again couldn't believe our fortune in being together. We were very pleased to reach the ranch and see the zebra, giraffe, and other wildlife roaming around. Just to watch it all together gave us great pleasure.

A few days later was Keith's birthday. We all went for a game drive around the ranch and came home for a sumptuous lunch. As a birthday present, I gave Keith a book on the early days in Kenya. He could learn something about the country he would possibly be coming to live in.

One morning Keith and I went for a flight with Father in our aircraft, the five-seater Navion. It was a great experience for Keith, who had never flown in a light aircraft before. The following week Keith and I left the ranch in my old Range Rover for Nairobi on our way to the coast. We stayed with friends of mine and left the following morning for Voi, stopping along the way for a picnic breakfast on the Athi-Kapiti Plains. Much later in the day we stopped at the Tsavo River, as I wanted to show Keith all the interesting places along the way. After a night in a safari camp, we continued all the way to Samsara, my property in the Shimba Hills. We had to get a number of things ready in the house and fix up the mosquito net after having made up the Arab-style bed.

Now, we were totally on our own and felt very relaxed and at ease together. During our time at Samsara, Keith fixed up more 12-volt wiring for the extra lights—pretty canal-boat lights—he had brought with him from the UK. One light was fixed in the bedroom and the other two in the attractive sitting room. It made an enormous difference to the house to have extra lights at night in addition to the candles, which were extremely romantic, but lights as well made it so much easier, particularly in the open-plan kitchen, where we had fixed a wall lamp.

On occasion we would drive down through coconut palm groves to Diani for shopping and to go to the beach.

One evening, I decided to make a really romantic meal for Keith and myself. I made all kinds of tasty little dishes and put a mattress covered with a lovely piece of deep-red material, with gold threads running through it, and lots of cushions outside the veranda. We had candlelight all around and we listened to a variety of our favourite music, while enjoying our meal with sparkling wine. As the evening grew late, we lay there beneath the full moon and twinkling stars and made passionate love, with all the deep feelings that were within us.

One day early in December wandering around Mombasa Old Town together, we entered some of the jewellery shops to have a look at what they had in stock. We found a sweet, little gold ring, studded with five zircons. Keith bought it and that evening while out to dinner at Ali Barbour's Restaurant at Diani Beach, Keith placed the ring on the third finger of my left hand, a token of our permanent friendship. We had another wonderful romantic evening, which we both enjoyed immensely, and afterwards we made our way back to Samsara and slipped into bed at eleven.

We enjoyed one another's company to the full for the rest of Keith's stay with me. We delighted in more wonderful and special evenings outside beneath the star-studded sky with candles burning, giving a gentle romantic glow, and listening to soft music. We drove to the beach and enjoyed picnics, walks, and lazing in the blue, warm waters of the Indian Ocean.

All too soon it was time for Keith to return to England. Our idyllic days and nights had come to an end. Our last evening together was so very beautiful and so very sad as we held one another close, so close, and talked more about our future and when we would meet again. We were not without tears as we sat together on the Samsara veranda, sipping wine and holding hands.

The morning of December 10th was upon us. Our love making was beautiful, but sadness overtook us as we lay in each other's arms. Keith told me that he would be back to see me in the coming March, another three months, so at least we could look forward to that time.

We left the house after a simple breakfast and slowly made our way to Mombasa Club. After lunch there, we retired to the room I had booked for myself for the night. We lay in each other's arms for some while, and then Keith dressed in long trousers and a casual shirt, ready for leaving. I put on my red Mexican dress; I wanted to look good for our last hour together. It was so terribly sad, and tears kept welling up in my eyes as we sat having a drink on the club veranda. Keith gently dabbed my tears with his handkerchief.

The taxi arrived at six in the evening to take Keith to the Mombasa airport. He was to fly to Nairobi and get the connection to the UK. We could hardly stand the unbearable pain of parting again. This time, after six wonderful weeks together, was the most painful experience. I was in a flood of tears; the wrench of parting was beyond words. As the taxi driver opened the car door for Keith to get in, Keith held me very close. Our last kiss, and his parting words were, "Until March, my darling."

A final squeeze and he was in the taxi driving out of the club car park. His last vision of me was a lonely figure in red, standing waving a last good-bye.

I felt unspeakably awful after Keith's departure. I wandered to the front of the club to gaze at the ocean through a sea of tears, and then went to sit in my room. It was so painful lying on the bed where we had both lain together. I lay and wept for what seemed an age. Late in the evening the phone rang: Keith had arrived in Nairobi and was ready to depart for England. I savoured his voice over the phone. I could hardly believe he wasn't with me in the room. I found it hard to accept the fact that he wouldn't be with me for another three months. It was all so terribly heart wrenching. We said good-bye over the phone, and I gently replaced the receiver onto its hook. From this moment we would both start to count the days, weeks, and months ahead.

I lay awake for a very long while, lonely and sad. I stroked the pillow next to me where Keith had lain earlier in the afternoon. Finally, in the early hours of the following morning, I fell asleep.

I awoke to deep loneliness and was thoroughly miserable.

Those six weeks now seemed like a dream out of paradise. I made my way back to Samsara. A terrible feeling of sad loneliness overcame me as I opened the kitchen door and walked inside, knowing that Keith was now all those thousands of miles away in England. I could not get used to the strange feeling. Was it really only yesterday that we stood together in each other's arms in this very kitchen, on this very spot where I was standing now? It felt like a lost dream. I wept my heart out for Keith, leaning against the shelves in the kitchen for support.

That night, I lay in my bed that I had shared for so many weeks feeling desperately sad and lonely. I could still smell the sweetness of him in the sheets and on his pillow, and I treasured this. Burying my face in his pillow, I cried until finally falling into a deep sleep of exhaustion.

A few days later, my mother and father came to Samsara to join me. This was a great relief, and it was wonderful to have their company. We spent some time together, and we were invited for Christmas with some friends.

During January, we came home to the ranch. Keith and I continued to write letters and faxes to each other and talked over the phone when possible. We felt that we were just so desperately missing each other, and it transpired during one of our phone conversations, that instead of Keith only coming for a period of three months in March and us having to part again, we would just "go for it" and plan to remain together in March, come what may. I put the phone down feeling a delightful warmth inside, knowing now that at long last we both had made the final decision. Our dream was now beginning to take place. We knew where we were heading. The date was made. Keith would arrive on the 11th of March. We were now looking ahead with great enthusiasm willing the days away, which seemed to be passing painfully slowly.

In the interim, I decided to design a house for our future. Father and I came to an area on the ranch where it would be possible to build a home, and I started to make drawings of a Mexican-style house and chose a site on which to build.

As the 11th of March drew closer, I was counting the days and hours, marking the days off my calendar each evening as I had done since Keith left. It was now days and hours rather than months and weeks to wait.

My parents and I went down to Nairobi in a convoy and stayed with friends in Langata outside of Nairobi. The morning of the eleventh arrived. I couldn't possibly have eaten any breakfast—I was far too excited. I dressed in a lightweight white blouse and a long Indian skirt, and then drove out to the airport counting the minutes until we would finally meet. His plane came in a little early, though he was a while getting his luggage through the customs area. I was standing amongst the crowd of craning necks that were trying to see through the glass doors to where all the passengers from two flights were coming through.

I thought I saw him, a figure taller than the rest, the familiar white mop of hair, but it was a little too far away to be sure. My heart was pounding with excitement, and then there he was, pushing the trolley with two large suitcases, a brief case, and other items.

We were in each other's arms. Oh, what utter joy at last after all the waiting and longing, and this time it would be forever and ever, never to part again …

The Building of Nirvana

Soon after Keith joined me, I showed him my house design and the area I had chosen to build. He was thrilled with the location and the design. We made a start by clearing the area, and then I showed two of the workers from the ranch how to dig a foundation. The next move was to make all our own building blocks, which I taught our workers how to do. We worked steadily but continuously. I had to teach the chaps everything, and together we built a substantial and very attractive Mexican-style home, with Moorish archways on the veranda and some on the inside, too. I am very interested in interior design, so had a lot of fun getting everything just the way we wanted it. Finances were short, but we did our best with what we had available. Keith put in the plumbing and the wiring for lights. He and I made all the roof trusses, quite an undertaking, but I gained a lot of knowledge from the huge home my father built on the ranch.

The main project took us over three years. We moved into the house in March 2000, and continued work on it after we were installed.

It was a happy time. There was still a lot of work to do, and the garden and patio areas took additional months to complete.

THE WEDDING

Having completed the building of Nirvana, Keith asked me to marry him, so, later that year, we started to organise for a small wedding. We chose September 2000.

I made my own wedding dress from a beautiful silk sari in a deep bluish purple and the head dress to go with it. The jewellery was amethyst, so everything matched well.

We were married at the Aberdare Country Club between the Aberdare Mountains and Mount Kenya, a beautiful location. The wedding took place outside on the grounds. We had around thirty guests, all friends from within Kenya. The music I chose was from the film *Lawrence of Arabia*, very romantic and moving.

Our honeymoon was four wonderful days in the Sarova Shaba Lodge, and in those marvellous surroundings it was most enjoyable. Even though we had many punctured tyres due to the rough terrain and a broken sump on the Range Rover, we were determined that all the vehicle problems would not spoil our honeymoon.

Returning home, we continued our interesting and loving life together, sometimes visiting my Samsara home in the Shimba Hills, other times visiting lodges and parks. We entertained from time to time and visited friends around the country. I continued to paint and run the home, and Keith would do outside jobs to keep things running.

We lived a very satisfying life for a number of years, twelve to be exact, and everything we did, we did together and enjoyed it that way, until there became a traumatic situation between Keith and his own immediate family.

Big disagreements were taking place between them, which, after some while, began to affect our marriage. I did everything possible to help to keep things the way they had always been for us, but Keith became more and more depressed with his family problems. Finally, he went back to the UK to get advice from medical people on his depression situation. He would be gone for months at a time, once it was nine months, and I realised that our marriage was becoming very unstable.

After his fifth and final visit to the UK, he never returned home. My dreams and the life I became accustomed to had come to an abrupt end. Life now stood still.

It took me three years to even accept the fact that I was on my own. My loved one was no longer with me. The dreams we had were now completely shattered.

As I write this story of my life, I have not seen Keith for eight years, although we are in touch by phone on rare occasions: birthdays, Christmases, and other special times.

Time, and only time, can help to heal shattered dreams and broken love. It takes many years to heal, but the scars remain for all time. They are always there. New dreams evolve. They don't replace the old dreams, but inevitably life goes on, and one clings to new hopes and new dreams.

Review Requested:
If you loved this book, would you please provide a
review at Amazon.com?

Lightning Source UK Ltd.
Milton Keynes UK
UKHW030659050219

336770UK00001B/90/P

9 781681 818504